YOU'RE GONNA LOVE IT

Chuck Lewis

Ten Speed Press

TEN SPEED PRESS
P.O. Box 7123
Berkeley, California 94707

Second Printing. First printing by:
    Hazelwood Press
    Post Office Box 991
    Stinson Beach, California 94970

Library of Congress Catalog Number: 85-2575
ISBN: 0-89815-142-2

Cover Design by Fred Dekker and Brenton Beck

Printed in the United States of America
10   9   8   7   6   5   4   3   2   1

To Virginia

Contents

Foreword

When two people decide to go to a movie and one wants a comedy while the other desires a tragedy, salesmanship is born. Even when one person decides to sacrifice and see the movie the other prefers, the sacrifice is an act of selling. They are silently saying, "See how nice I am to you?" The next day the seller of the movie finds himself doing something the sacrificer desires. It all works out. Everybody is a salesman.

But it is a paradox, for many persons deny their salesmanship, like a doctor I met socially who said, "I could never be a salesman." I wondered how all those gall bladder operations occurred. Maybe his patients came rushing through his door shouting, "Cut me! Cut me!" When I asked, he smiled and we had a better conversation going in a few seconds.

My father claims he tried selling once and couldn't do it and so became an accountant. He defines his fine people manners, excellent service and conscientious attention to other people's details by the bland word "accounting." A misnomer.

My cousin Tom is a dentist. I sat in his chair once and his easygoing smile was more reassuring than the chrome plating on his expensive gadgets. He is a salesman as surely as is my dad.

1

Some people say they do not care to sell and will just take what they want. A few go to the extreme of doing this in liquor stores at the point of a gun. That seems very persuasive to me. But now and then a little grey-haired lady will reach under the counter with a quick hand and pull out a .38 and plug the non-salesman who thought he had an irresistible appeal. Everyone has their own level of sales resistance and some days work is a drag.

What many people seem to be saying in the denial of their salesmanship is that they do not want to be pictured as a manipulator of others. But if they never sell yet still get their way sometimes it would have to figure that they are gods, offering exactly what the other person desires at the moment. That seems unlikely.

Parents are the most natural salespersons in the world and yet they prove the erratic fallibility of the god stance in influencing their children. I have an honorary Jewish Mother in Atlanta who will make me a bowl of chicken soup at my first sign of a sniffle. That soup has more love in it than any other dish in the world. I call it Jewish penicillin. She says her mother, who gave her the recipe for it, is a strong salesperson and is also the official Southeastern distributor of guilt.

Many people do not like to be pictured as salespersons for that reason, the implied injection of emotion into others. Selling, from this viewpoint, appears to be a harangue and a hassle. Sometimes it is if the salesperson erroneously perceives and accepts selling as a challenge of swaying other people's opinions against their will.

But mainly what I hear beneath all the denials of salesmanship is a fear of not doing it very well and a desire to improve without harming either the other person or self. That is what this book is all about, selling without harm.

Because you are stuck with your natural salesmanship anyway and couldn't get rid of it if you tried, why not read on and improve it?

I'll make you a promise. You will not have to influence anyone to do anything they do not really want to do.

CHAPTER 1

Fishermen, Peddlers and Karma

In a marine dealership where I was sales manager a man walked in and started talking before I could even say "hello."

"I want one of those fishing boats with the high swivel seats and one of those jacket patches that says BASS on it."

I knew why he wanted the boat because it was the same reason he wanted the patch, which is the membership insignia of the "Bass Anglers Sportsman's Society." He wanted to belong, to imitate, to join the fraternity of liars known as fishermen.

As I showed him a rig better than the medium grade I talked about the fun of fishing with your buddies. He wanted that fun so that's what we talked about and the boat just came along in the whole deal along with a coupon to mail in to join BASS and get his patch.

The first rule of selling is to talk about anything at all if it is what interests the customer and leads to a sale. This man had never fished or been boating in his life. Any real detailed talk about boats might have just confused him.

Considering fishermen brings us to a good point in salesmanship.

While all fishermen are liars, and even Billy Graham couldn't accurately describe the size of the last fish he caught, the salesman who lies is in trouble. When a fisherman tells me the panfish were running a pound apiece, I know he caught some three-quarter pound fish. If he had said three-quarters he would know I would believe it to be half a pound. So he tells me one pound and knows I know what he really caught.

A salesman who worked with the same industrial company as I did years ago couldn't keep his fishing and sales stories separated. He sold like a fisherman. Because I had to relate to those same customers, I challenged him on it. He gave me the fisherman's logic, "Nobody believes a salesman, so you have to tell them four times more than the truth so when they discount three-fourths of it there is still enough left to make them want to buy." This fellow would tell a lie even when the truth would do a better job.

There is a small problem involved with this method. When a fish is smaller than stated no one is harmed unless they were counting on it for dinner, so most fishermen wait until the fish is eaten to begin the story stretching. But when a salesman lies it is up front and the customer is counting on what he heard. When it doesn't materialize later the customer is hungry, usually for blood.

Another big difference is that fish lies only involve a few ounces or inches of uniform commodity, the fish. But sales appeals cover a lot of different points and appeal to a lot of emotions. My co-worker never knew which parts the customer was discounting and which parts he was believing as he decided to buy. As a result the customer usually had a valid reason to become unhappy later.

The scales balance out. Fishermen hate scales but a good salesman loves them. A fair measure can stand a close examination. Gurus recently capturing the American eye have a word for this principle.

The word in the balancing of scales is "Karma." People

say, "What goes around comes around," meaning if a person cheats someone he will in turn be cheated by someone else later, or if the punishing act is not identical it will at least be as severe.

But Karma is more than that, more direct, and there is no lost time in it coming back, for Karma is not what you get back, it is what you become. You become what you do. When a new prospect will not buy a product from a dubious looking salesman it is usually because too many others already have.

The Karma in selling means simply that if a person lies he begins to look and feel like a liar and finds fewer and fewer people believing, and ends up doubting himself. In this way today's fast buck comes back as tomorrow's starvation, if not financially, at least emotionally.

I learned all this Karma business from my grandfather when I was eight years old and sold vegetables with him from a truck in the summer. The first lesson came the first day when I measured a peck of potatoes for a customer. When I brought it to my grandfather he looked at it, smiled at the customer, then at me, and said, "Son, that isn't a peck of potatoes. It's just full." Then he heaped more potatoes on top until they formed a pyramid, making it really about a peck and a fourth. Next, I flunked beans by measuring them carefully up to the two pounds requested, dropping them in the scale a few at a time until the scale pointer hit the two mark. Another smile and another handful of beans made it come up to grandfather's two pounds even though the pointer was halfway to the three.

When we got back in the truck cab I asked him if he wasn't giving his stuff away. My grandfather never took the Dale Carnegie personality course, but he could have taught it.

"When you give something extra people don't worry about the old scales being hairline accurate. Maybe they're not. I don't know and it doesn't matter. If we give them good measure they know they are getting enough. Where it really pays off is when we sell watermelons."

I didn't know exactly what he meant until the melons at last came to the market from Georgia. Then the first customer asked, "Are they good and ripe?" Grandfather, who usually had something funny to say, like, "Tender as a mother's love" about the yellow corn, just stood quietly when asked about the watermelons.

"I guarantee them."

Bingo! One watermelon sold. And he was as good as his word. The next time we stopped he remembered and made it a casual point to ask, "How was the watermelon?" The reply was always, "Great!" and everyone smiled. One day a lady said, "A little over-ripe." Grandfather reached over, picked the best looking melon off the shelf, handed it to me without one word to the customer and said, "Put this up on the porch for Mrs. Smith, son." As I walked away I could hear her protesting that it wasn't that bad and him saying it only had to be a little bad to qualify for the guarantee. Then with a smiling, mock reproach he said, "Please don't tell me how to run my vegetable truck."

I asked him another question when we drove away and he said,

"Some things come one at a time and you can't tell a good one from a bad one for sure until you taste it. We guarantee the eating. Some other things come by pounds and we don't know exactly how good those scales are. We make sure they are good enough. Other things come by the peck and we give them all the peck can hold. But do you notice all the stuff we sell by the dozen, or three for a quarter, or one at a time besides watermelons? Those things pay for the watermelon guarantee and the extra beans and potatoes. It all fits together. You notice how the customers seem to like it all? It's all good. That little bit extra just lets them know how good it is. Also, it makes you feel good to give them a little extra. Any more questions?"

"Nope."

Karma is not what comes back. It is what a person becomes.

The beautiful part of Karma is that it is totally controllable. Because the rule of Karma is, "What goes around comes around," all a person has to do to get something back is first send it around. We get what we are what we do. If a good Karma is desired just do something good. There is no waiting time for the reward. It is received at the same time it is given.

At first this appears to be a gamble. By giving something of value there is a risk the other person will not respond with an equal value. Here is where Karma is misunderstood by the person who gives mindlessly to the extent that it becomes damaging to self in a sacrificing way. O.K., the danger is that the other person will not give back. So let's call it a gamble. All of life is a gamble. But there is a reasonable way to gamble. Just bet your stakes in amounts that are affordable. A dice player with a stake of $100.00 can bet in one of two ways, either by rolling the dice one time for the entire stake or by betting five or ten dollars at a time.

Emotionally, give what is affordable and never forget to give yourself consideration even as you give to another person so you can stop before you give the whole store away. Also, always remember that Karma is an internal force. While surface actions and a true balance in give and take situations cannot always be achieved, the inner Karma is always hairline accurate. We get what we are what we do.

Let's take a look at Karma in an updated situation.

The Hewitt-Robbins Company had just built a new plant in Columbia, South Carolina to manufacture huge rock crushing machines. They had two immediate problems: one, the transfer of production from their main facility in Milwaukee, and, two, a change in engineering within the product. Previously the machines had been powered with electric motors. New models were to be powered by hydraulics. This meant out with the electric wires and in with hose lines.

I called on them to sell the hydraulic hose and fittings and introduced myself to the buyer.

"Hose and fittings? You are too late, my friend. Engineering placed a material request when we redesigned our power over to hydraulics from electric power. Milwaukee purchasing ordered the hose and fittings and they arrived here before the people did. No, we have a lot of new problems here but hose and fittings isn't one of them. Sorry."

(Lost? What do you think? Take a second look at that last comment. "Problems.")

"What brand did you receive?"

"Parker-Hannifin."

"Great! Fine outfit. Good products. By the way, isn't this your company's first experience with hydraulics?"

"Yes."

"Who is going to install them?"

"The men on the assembly line."

"Did they come here from Milwaukee?"

"No, we are hiring locally."

"That's funny."

"What do you mean?"

"Well, I work with everyone in this area who uses hydraulics. You see, hydraulic hose and fittings are a technically exact procedure. If they are assembled or installed incorrectly they will not hold up to the extreme pressures in the hydraulic system. If a fitting blows off or a hose bursts there is havoc. The machine is down and if someone is standing in the wrong place at the instant of failure they can be injured. Parker's products and my products will each hold up to the job, but only if they are installed correctly. But the main thing I'm concerned about is simply that because I work closely with all the manufacturers in this area I know all the experienced assemblymen. The last time I noticed, they were all still on their jobs. The overwhelming odds are that none of your men know how to install the hose lines. Why don't you check this out on the intercom with your production foreman?"

"I guess I'd better."

He called the foreman and discovered I was right. Then I gave him a more detailed explanation of exactly how our product was constructed, how it worked, then offered to supply him with my hose and work with his men to ensure that correct procedures were being followed. He stated he would have to use up the Parker products, and that he would just get the Parker rep to come in and teach his men.

"O.K. But would you mind a suggestion?"

"No. What is it?"

"Well, Parker is a good outfit, but they spread their men too thin. I live just four miles from your plant, but Parker's rep lives in Atlanta and covers three or four states. They are running ninety miles an hour. If I were you I would phone them this instant. I'll wait. You may need me yet."

He phoned and couldn't get the help in time from

Parker. But he still had their product on hand.

"Look, I'd like to do business with you, but I have to use up that Parker hose."

"I wish I could help you there, but I can't. I would not want to be responsible for instructing your men about a product I do not understand as thoroughly as I do my own. If something went wrong you would hold me responsible. But we can still do business together."

"How?"

"No problem. Give me an open purchase order number and a set of your blueprints. I'll order in the necessary inventory, then instruct your men. First, we will hold a classroom clinic. Second, we will go to your shop and each man will actually practice assembling the hose lines. Third, I will personally supervise your men on the assembly line to further assist them and ensure that no mistakes are made."

He gave me the purchase order and the blueprints. That first order totalled approximately six thousand dollars.

Two aftermaths of this work. One, after I instructed his men how to use my product they understood it, while the Parker products were still a mystery. As a result, two years later the Parker inventory was still on the shelves gathering dust and the assemblymen refused to use it up even when so instructed by the plant manager. They said they didn't understand how to use that brand of hose and fittings. Meanwhile, my company kept on getting the flow of repeat orders.

Second, I got some Karma in the form of a satisfactory commission and also in two surprise letters to my company. Take a look at these letters. They represent the essence of selling—customer satisfaction and a fair profit to the seller.

Aeroquip Corporation
Industrial Division
300 S. East Avenue
Jackson, Michigan 49023

ATTENTION: Sales Manager

Gentlemen:

This is a special letter of appreciation to Mr. Chuck Lewis, Senior Sales Engineer of Aeroquip Corporation for his time and efforts in assisting us at Hewitt-Robbins, BHO, Columbia, in the hydraulic piping of our first plant to be built in our new facility.

Mr. Lewis conducted a well presented training seminar for our Assembly Department and has devoted his time and skill in the actual work of piping up this plant. I would like to express my sincere thanks to Mr. Lewis on behalf of all of us in the Manufacturing Group of Hewitt-Robbins, Columbia.

Sincerely,

HEWITT-ROBBINS, INC.

(signed)

John E. Frawley
Production Superintendent

President, Aeroquip Corporation
Industrial Division
300 S. East Avenue
Jackson, Michigan 49203

Dear Sir:

Every now and then an event takes place which is out of the ordinary, and that is impossible to go unnoticed by many people. We at Hewitt-Robbins have for the past several weeks been in the process of completing our first major portable process plant at our new facilities here in Columbia, South Carolina.

With somewhat inexperienced personnel, we have experienced many normal start-up problems. One area in which this has not taken place is due solely to the outstanding efforts of your Senior Sales Engineer, Chuck Lewis. Chuck has spent many hours of personal time "getting his hands dirty," helping us complete the hydraulic system on this plant.

His efforts should not go unnoticed. You can be proud to have this man as a member of your organization.

Sincerely,

(signed)

H.E. Schmidt
Manager Industrial Relations

Now, granted, those letters talk about the hydraulic business in South Carolina, and maybe you are in the business of selling jump ropes to schoolgirls in Minnesota.

But if that kind of customer satisfaction is what you desire in your sales efforts, would you be interested in learning how to read situations that accurately and sell that effectively?

You would? Great! Read on.

Now that you can see the customer's total satisfaction with the sale, let's go back and analyze exactly what was happening in my presentation.

First, I already knew all the answers to all the questions I asked that buyer. But questions capture the attention of people. When they answer, they have to think first. When they think, they accept their own ideas and facts. In other words, he told himself he was about to have some difficulty. Always try to let the other person tell themselves everything you want them to know. Ask questions that lead to their self-instruction. Before you start, find out all the answers, if possible. Then you can ask the questions in the proper sequence. It beats a lecture.

Second, take a look at the buyer and his emotions. His sentence gave me the clue I needed to form the right emphasis for him as he understood himself. "We have a lot of problems, but hose and fittings isn't one of them." He identifies himself as a problem solver right there. So what's the best thing to hand a problem solver? You've got it. A problem. Notice how the statement "Hose and fittings are a technically exact procedure" loads the air with the beginnings of concern? The word "procedure" nearly becomes a verb. Most nouns are words that sit there like the hose and fittings on his shelves. But the word "procedure" moves along in the mind, becoming one of his problems. In actual fact, his facial expression changed to one of concern as he absorbed that sentence.

This buyer took pride in doing his job well, solving problems. He became aware of the problem and desired to handle it correctly. He desired my knowledge and was eager to imitate all those other quality manufacturers with whom I worked closely.

Next, I didn't "sell" him. How could I have? Didn t he already have a full inventory of hose and fittings bulging his shelves? No. I just held up a few of his own priorities for him to see and he purchased. His priorities were the standard four buying motives: pride, awareness of hazard, desire for gain, and imitation. Finally, yes, there was some leading of the buyer to my conclusion. If you want to you can call it manipulation. Also, if you desire, you can assign some negative value to one person manipulating another. But what is the alternative? Re-read the letters from the customer. Seems to me he got a pretty good deal by my manipulating him. Also, I merely asked questions. His answers led him to the purchase.

In all equitable selling there is a fairness and an exchange of values. The secret to a decent transaction is one simple question. Did everyone involved walk away from it smiling?

CHAPTER 2

Fear Versus Awareness

In fear of failure a buyer may reach for a product as a way of running from disaster. When this happens often the disaster is magnified beyond any realistic reasonable estimate. Or in search of quality the buyer may reach for some very pleasant positives, creating an awareness of well being and just incidentally, without undue concern, avoiding the existing hazard or the negative consideration.

Let's examine this principle by looking at a specific product. I've chosen automobile shock absorbers as the product because I am totally familiar with them. As the story unfolds we will not only examine fear versus commitment to quality, but will also, and of greater importance, examine the choices a salesman has in his moods in dealing with people.

Shock absorbers perform a very desirable and necessary function in an automobile by absorbing tire bounce and dampening the vehicle's up and down motion, keeping the tires firmly on the road surface, reducing stopping distances because the tires cannot break free to skip up in the air when brakes are applied. On curves, shock absorbers provide a slip-free firm footing and reduce sway and lean, resulting in a very fine ride. This means an older car will often ride better than a new car if the older car has the better shock absorbers.

What is the best way to sell this product? Talk about the danger of worn shocks? Or present a demonstration of the positive aspects of the product?

For four years prior to selling hydraulic hose and fittings, I sold Monroe-Matic shock absorbers in the Carolinas as a factory salesman. A good portion of sales volume was gained through merchandising programs. First, a big central warehouse distributor was selected to stock the product. A smaller inventory was stocked by the local automotive parts jobber.

Periodically, all factory salesmen were called in to the home office at a big sales meeting and given a new merchandising program aimed directly to the motorist by first capturing the attention of the men who serviced the cars. As an example, one year each jobber was given a beautiful shotgun to use as a prize for the dealer in his town who sold the most shock absorbers. The five highest selling dealers in my zone were taken to Monroe's luxurious hunting lodge in Michigan to enjoy three days of excellent duck and pheasant hunting.

To participate in the program, the jobber was required to hold a dealer meeting and allow me to give his dealers a sales presentation, then make personal calls with the jobber's salesmen to enlist the dealers, one at a time. The dealer, to participate, purchased a smaller stock and was given a demonstrator unit with good and bad shocks mounted on a barrel which was painted with advertising.

One funny aspect of that particular year's program was that it provided a tool to focus some laughs on the interplay between buyer and seller when I carried the shotgun in with me to present the program.

"Today, Jim, I get a very big order, or else."

Or, if the customer spoke first—

"Don't shoot! I'll buy whatever you are selling."

And over a few intercoms—

"Chuck Lewis is here to see you, and it looks like he means business."

And on one missed sale—

"Go ahead and shoot. I ain't buying anything today."

One adage of selling is "That which holds attention determines action" and I certainly gained some very good attention as I walked in with that shotgun.

One quick trip through my territory scheduled all the jobbers for sales meetings and follow-up dealer work. Then the meetings were held according to the schedule.

As an enticement in inviting the dealer's attendance, I showed a film of the most recent Indianapolis 500 mile race, produced specifically for the merchandising meeting campaign by Monroe.

Finally, all this accomplished, shotgun in hand, I approached the dealer in his service station garage, alignment and brake shop, or tire dealership. Now past the type of selling that concentrates on motivating wholesale merchants toward profitable sales efforts, I was face to face with retail dealers and motorists who needed to know about shock absorbers and what they did for the car.

A good way to induce the dealer was to sell one of his customers as he watched. At this point, the shotgun and the profit became incidental to the basic question of the value of the shock absorber to the car and the driver. And bear in mind that shock absorbers wear out so gradually that the deteriorated ride is not a suddenly noticed experience. As the car slowly begins riding rougher the driver slowly adjusts to it, gradually driving the car slower, braking more cautiously, considering a trade-in for a better riding car, not knowing new shock absorbers are the key to satisfaction with his present car or even really understanding the real hazards of his car's present condition.

Now what should I do? Sell the fear or the desire and commitment to quality? At this point it was not an idle philosophical debate. With a family to support and a quota to reach, I determined to sell whichever way produced the most results. This was my first good sales job and I was full of a need to prove myself and willing to make the sale regardless of what was required. Sounds calloused, doesn't it? Maybe it was. Or maybe it was just eagerness. I'm not going to attack it or defend it. It was a time of my life when I was searching hard. Some of it had to be erroneous mixed in with the good.

Some of the company advertising leaned toward fear. One consumer ad pictured just a man's two hands and a wallet. One hand held the wallet open while the other hand dipped into the folding money compartment. The money was visible, half way out of the wallet. In the plastic window of the wallet was a family snapshot of a charming wife and two beautiful children. The ad caption was, "Sure, you can buy a cheaper shock absorber. But the only thing you will save is money." The Monroe logo and a picture of a shock absorber completed the ad.

Part of me felt like a crusader, saving my customers from the dangers of worn shock absorbers. When I listened too hard to this inner voice I sold by discussing the dangers of worn shocks. But another part of me thoroughly enjoyed riding in my company car which was equipped with four load levelers. A load leveler is a shock absorber with a coil spring included. The stability provided by these units was unbelievable and driving that car was an extraordinarily pleasant experience.

To demonstrate this pleasure, I gave test rides to any who would ride. First, after my passengers were seated in the car, I asked to be directed to the roughest road or country lane in the area. On the way, if we drove on some rural roads, I steered the right wheels two feet out into the rough road shoulder and let the speed get up to fifty. This is an eye-opening experience, for the car remained stable and level when passengers just knew we should be fishtailing or crashing into a field at any moment. As we sped along I asked, "See how smooth this ride is?" as I steered with two fingers on the wheel. Finally getting to the rough stretch, often a stretch with broken pavement, I said, "I will deliberately aim for every pothole I can find." Next I advised everyone to brace for a sudden stop, then slammed on the brakes, hard. The superior traction and level control stopped the car in a surprisingly short distance, dead straight in its tracks without dipping sharply in the front end. The finale came when I ferreted out a railroad crossing and asked what speed they usually used crossing it. A typical verbal exchange was, "Slow down! That crossing is rough as a cob! Five miles an hour is all it will take." Then my, "Really? Let's try it at thirty miles an hour." After my prospects unwrapped their arms from their heads, recovering from their fright and surprise of crossing smoothly instead of being thrown through the roof, they often got out back at the station and became instant customers.

Before we go further, you are hoping that I can get some humility. Driving people around like that in those demonstration rides sort of leaves you with the impression that I was riding a little too high. You're right. As it says in the Book, "Pride goeth before destruction, and a haughty spirit precedeth a fall."

In a small North Carolina town, a dealer agreed to a test ride. As we pulled out of his Shell service station he enthusiastically asked me to take a certain route out of town. After doing the wheels-on-the-shoulder part of the demonstration he had me circle around to a road that approached the town from the east. Some curves ahead prompted me to ask, "How fast do you take those curves?" He said, "Seventy." I settled for that figure. Usually I would add fifteen miles to the passenger's stated speed, but seventy seemed fast enough. When we were committed well into the first curve to the right I realized my passenger was either a daredevil or a liar. Even with the great load levelers the pull of the curve forced the car to grab the road in a hairline balance between control and crash. Coming out of the curve into a very short straight section I braked as much as I dared to get ready for the next curve. Forget selling anything. I was hoping to survive. Going into the next curve to the left I had to accelerate to gain traction and control. Again the seat of my pants advised we were on a fine edge. Making it through that curve I wanted to congratulate myself, but an approaching narrow bridge influenced me to delay the celebration because another curve lay between us and the bridge. Finally, either the car or my nerves were not equal to the task and the end concrete pillar on the right side of the bridge was coming at the exact center of the front bumper at about sixty miles per hour. In absolute desperation I yanked the wheel hard to the left, then snatched it hard back to the right. The car crabbed sideways to enter the bridge, but coming back to the right I oversteered and the right headlight and bumper dug into the bridge railing, stripping some chrome from the car, spinning us around where we finished the ride through the bridge backwards, fastened to our seats by safety belts and pinched nerves.

An eighteen wheel trucker had seen our carom approach and stopped before entering the bridge toward us. As we stopped exactly even with its cab the big, grinning driver leaned down and said, "Great show! What you fellows going to do next?"

"Go pick up our chrome."

But before we could run out on the bridge to retrieve the metal my passenger said,

"Damn! These load levelers are terrific! I've tried that three times and wrecked three cars!"

When we got back to his Shell station, bent chrome stacked in the back seat, I took a close look at what I should have noticed before we departed on our ride. There in the window and on his shelves was a very good assortment of racing trophies. This fellow was a daredevil!

We took turns using the phone. He called his buddies.

"Joe. Get your car over here quick! I've got the damnedest stabilizers to install in it that you ever dreamed about. Wait till you see."

While I assessed my car damage he sold a complete merchandising package of my product over the telephone.

When I finally phoned my office to report the mishap and they discovered it was during a customer test ride they were aghast. Bob Rye, Monroe's genial chief accountant and insurance administrator, was particularly appalled.

"But Bob, this fellow is now the most enthusiastic dealer in the South."

Bob wasn't impressed. Sometimes accountants don't have much sense of humor.

So O.K., I've been taken down a notch. Am I more human now?

When I decided on an arbitrary basis to sell shock absorbers by emphasizing the danger of the worn shocks, I cited examples of accidents which were caused by the faulty equipment. One tool I used was a clipped newspaper article describing a fatal accident. In this write-up a sheriff made the statement that worn out shock absorbers were directly responsible for the fatality. I emphasized the danger and counted on the customer to feel the fear and purchase new shock absorbers. I made sales.

But I got bored. I felt like the voice of doom and got tired of it. Actually, the negatives were getting to me as much as the customers. I was frowning a lot. It didn't agree with my nature, which is to use a good bit of humor with people.

Then I switched over to talking about the great ride characteristics of my product. This was better. I could discuss surefooted turning, smooth riding, effortless braking. I gave even more test rides where formerly I had been wearing out that newspaper article showing it and creating fear. Now I was smiling all the time. Great!

I thought I had it made. Look! I can sell fear or cheer and make a living, and I alone can select the mood! Terrific! I must be dynamite! A real traveling salesman! A road running smooth mouth.

Some of my prospects, the ones with studious looks, began evading their responsibility, which in my mind was simply to become customers. I wondered why this was happening. Couldn't they see the greatness of the product? I used ever increasing accolades as I described the product. Hollywood would have been proud of me. It's great! It's magnificent! It's stupendous! No sale.

Then I looked again at those who refused to purchase, still trying to figure it out to see if there was a pattern. First, I dismissed from my mind those who said they were about to trade their car, those who were broke, and those whose present shock absorbers were marginal, not so good, but still not totally worn out. This left me with just those who had totally worn out shock absorbers on cars they planned to drive a good while longer. My enthusiasm was not convincing some of those in this group who were studious looking, or the quiet ones.

So I switched back to fear-injection tactics. I didn't like the doomsday approach, but I went back to it when the enthusiastic bit didn't work. But also, now I was in the habit of noticing how some people wouldn't purchase. Back in the doomsday sales pitch I still missed selling some people. But now instead of the quiet, studious ones, I began missing the smiling, laughing ones.

Nuts! Either way I worked it I missed some sales I should have made. Finally I asked myself, "What is it going to take to sell these people?" I had used up all my resources. So I looked at my customers even harder. When I did, I got my answer. Everybody wants something different. The quiet, studious ones wanted to avoid hazards, but the smiling, laughing people just wanted the pleasure of the ride.

The solution? Give each one of them what he wanted. This meant that I had to throw away my predetermined mood and couldn't get up Monday morning and determine to be just enthusiastic or just fear-injecting all week long. I was going to meet some who wanted safety and others who wanted pleasure.

So now I had two separate sales pitches: cheer or fear. All I had to do was look for smilers or frowners. This began to work a little better. This should be the end of the story, right? Wrong. Is anything ever that easy? I began to discover some smilers who smiled to cover up their inner fears, and some frowners who were really quite cheerful people who were just concerned about something at the moment. Ah! Would the human race please slow down so I could make a living?

The real problem in meeting people is that some of them do not give me their entire set of signals when we shake hands and say "hello." O.K. Have it your way, friends. I'd already given up on having it my way.

All this sounds very glib later, in print. But when you are out there nose-to-nose with a lot of people who are supposed to make you feel good by buying something, you know, pay your rent, feed your kids, and make you believe you really are a worthwhile person of some ability, it isn't a tea dance when it doesn't happen. It is a fumbling, stumbling, error productive experience, loaded with self-doubts. And sometimes the frustration causes a more determined attempt the next time. Then the cheer sales pitch comes out as, "It's great! (dammit!)" The fear pitch becomes, "If you don't buy this you will probably be dead by noon tomorrow!" Are you beginning to see the frustration level in it?

So I began looking at people in detail instead of sales pitches. Being so frustrated with ineffective sales pitches, and also frustrated with my frustration, I turned loose of all of it. For a while I was like a whipped dog. I couldn't sell. For a period of time I fed my family just by moving fast and getting in front of so many people that the natural buyers were contacted. Humility. I carried a truck load of it with me daily. But the way I spelled it it came out I-N-C-O-M-P-E-T-E-N-C-E. I could not sell at all. But I still had to eat, so I went out every day looking for buyers, moved fast, and found them. Operating this way required a resigned form of optimism. Even a blind hog finds an occasional acorn.

I've got a problem. A natural curiosity. I ask, "Why?" a lot. I began asking myself why these people purchased from me. Before, I had asked why I wasn't selling them, but then when I didn't get an answer I had given up on selling anything at all. But still the old question, "Why?" was important to me. So alright, if you people are buyers, why? And those of you who don't buy, why?

The Book says, "Seek and ye shall find." It is true of all human endeavor. If you do not believe this, see how much finding you achieve without seeking. When you accidentally stumble across some valuable thing you will not recognize its value and will walk right by it. The other part of this "Seek and Find" truth is the part that always frustrates everybody, for no directions are given on just where to look. The Book just says, "Seek."

I began looking at people in even more detail, searching. I'm not a psychologist, just a working salesman, but I began watching people very intently to discover what made them choose as they did.

A young man with a souped-up car insisted upon a little decal to put in his car window: "Equipped with Monroe-Matic Shock Absorbers." He didn't buy the shock absorbers yet. That would happen next payday, but he talked me out of a decal. When he put it in place in the window his chest swelled up. Proud as a peacock.

An older man questioned me at length about the increased tire mileage and the increased protection of alignment and front end steering parts. When he thought it all over out loud he figured he would save money by having new shock absorbers. He wanted an advantage, a gain of some sort.

A lady with a troubled look asked if it would help her car avoid swaying so terribly on mountain roads. Her purchase was because of an increasing awareness of a hazard.

And finally, there were people who purchased because their friends had purchased and they wanted to keep up with the Joneses. The Carolinians were very car conscious because of all the big name racers who lived and raced there.

It all sifted down to four main reasons for buying:

Pride of ownership

Desire for gain

Awareness of existing hazard or potential danger

Imitation

But still these customers were holding out on me at first sight. Oh, some of them were easy to read, but most of them had learned how to act neutral, noncommittal. They shook my hand, said hello, and then stood quietly waiting for me to speak. None of them actually said, "I'm a sucker for imitating my friends," or, "I'm scared to death most of the time and if you show me some danger I'll buy anything." No, they just stood there.

As a result of my looking to them to buy instead of myself to sell, combined with them acting so vague at first, I lost all my preconceived notions. I would begin talking about the product or the customer's car or the dealer's business in a very tentative way. As I talked, I watched these people to see if they agreed with some of my statements.

There is a strange quality about talking to people this way, without a totally firm script. An emptiness occurs inside. When I had no absolute knowledge of what to say next, it was a fumbling experience. But then I began making an unbelievable number of sales. For those who feel that comparative figures are the only proof of the pudding, consider these. My territory was South Carolina, a state which at that time had an economy so low on the national scale that only Mississippi's per capita income was lower. Yet at the dealer level I outsold the other men in my zone which consisted of North Carolina and Virginia, each with much greater sales potential. (Why is it that only big is considered good?)

Also, often I went into North Carolina and Virginia to assist the other salesmen on large sales programs where a lot of jobber salesmen needed sales assistance at the same time. We called it a Blitz—four salesmen in one town at one time. My co-workers played a trick on me which I was too inexperienced to realize. Sorting through the schedule, they set themselves up to work with the hottest salesman in town and assigned me to work with the salesman who they didn't feel was quite as sharp, and therefore didn't have as thorough an acceptance with his dealer customers. Because I was too ignorant to realize what they were doing, or that my assigned salesman wasn't as sharp as the one they worked with, I went out for the day's work all simple minded and came back with more orders than they did. Finally after two years they admitted it while we were having a beer session one night.

But the ignorance was paying off in front of the prospects. I didn't think I was much of a salesman and I was looking for them to purchase my product instead of myself to sell it. I was empty of a guaranteed winner appeal. But prospects were buying from me like crazy. I'd stand there and ying and yang back and forth with the prospect, being very, very careful not to irritate them until they made up their mind to buy. And there would be this lull or blockage point that would look like it would kill the momentum. From somewhere inside, right in the middle of that empty feeling, would come some remark, formed internally. When I let the remark out, it moved the sale along.

For four years I worked like that, gut empty, my mind a complete blank when an obstacle cropped up in the sales conversation. And about every time, this inner remark would form. Well, if it works, use it. I relaxed. I could walk in, begin a very polite sales presentation and just see what happened next, listen to the inner voice, and make a sale.

Sometimes I fought it, and tried to overpower people right up front. It never worked. I had to let them present an obstacle of their choosing, then soothe their concern or solve their problem with a comment formed instantly within.

The other way, being a big-shot up front, never worked. Once, all full of myself, I purchased two expensive cigars and gave one to my selling buddy of the day. We lighted up, then feeling very grand about our image we walked into a garage in a small town, cigars stuck up in our faces. The prospect said, "Must be fixin' to rain." The day was blazing hot without a cloud in sight. I asked, "Why do you say that?" He replied, "'Cause the hogs are runnin' around with sticks in their mouths." No sale.

But often it was funny how a sale could be made the other way, not overpowering anyone. One dealer told me the instant we walked in, "I don't want to hear any sales pitch today." He didn't look angry, just tired. I said, "O.K. I'll put my notebook back in the car and wait for Joe here to check your usual stock items." When I came back from the car empty handed I had a drink of water, then stood quietly in the station's service room. I started feeling the man's tiredness. After a few minutes, I said, "Hot, isn't it?" "Yep." Then I settled into a very relaxed wait. Not for Joe to finish checking the stock but for this fellow to get his curiosity up. Finally he asked, "What are you selling?" I said, "Just a minute," went out, got my notebook and went in again. He purchased. He had begun thinking about his mood, and my, "Hot, isn't it?" display of sympathy. Plus, his curiosity was hooked because he couldn't figure out how a salesman would let him off the hook that easy. Maybe a salesman wouldn't have.

There is a saying, "You have to be one to see one." Here are a few more examples. I can find myself in these customers. In fact, I did find myself in them in order to make the sale. Excuse me. There I go again thinking I'm a salesman. In order for them to buy from me.

On another call, before going into a station, the jobber salesman cautioned me that the prospect was a very loud wise mouth. When we pulled up in the car the dealer looked out his window and I could see his mouth moving. Then I saw six loafers in there laughing at whatever he had said about us in our car all painted up with advertising. Before we got out I asked the jobber salesman, "Will you help me with this fellow?"

"How?"

"Well, I don't know what I'm going to say and he appears to want to wise crack, so how about you and I just saying nothing at all until some of his remarks give me some time to think. Will you just be real quiet and smile, no matter what he says?"

"O.K."

We went in, and the first wise crack hit us before the door closed. "Well, I see we've got a real live factory expert salesman here. Probably come to show us mechanics how to get rich."

The six guys laughed again. We remained silent and smiled. "Must be nice, ride around in a new car, eating high on the hog on an expense account."

More laughter. This was a show he was putting on for the loafers, at our expense. His voice was sharp and strident. He was stuffed full of pride. He cracked a few more severe lines at us, his peer group laughed, and we stood there taking it all in with a smile. The comments got worse because he needed some feedback to keep the fire going. He tried to hook us in, but we remained silent. Finally, he ran out of words.

"What do you guys want?"

"Well, I've heard all over town that you can fix anything on a car and that you are a good dealer. I also heard you can sell and you have enough courage to buy. I asked Joe here to bring me by to see if the story I heard was true or false. As you can see from our car advertising we are selling Monroe shock absorbers. A barrel full of them contains shocks and load levelers for just three cars, a Ford, a Chevy and a Plymouth. Now how about it? Was the story I heard just a lot of crap, or can you handle a deal this size?"

Every eye in the place snapped from my face to his. He turned red.

"Hell yes. I can handle anything."

"Great! We'll deliver this afternoon. Thanks!"

Two seconds later we were out the door.

That kind of selling relates to marketing as stunt flying does to aviation, and just as daredevils crash, "Fast Eddies" often take to strong drink. I couldn't take ten calls a day like that one or I'd get so sickened on human nature's negatives, including mine, that I would have to drink a lot.

Let's look at one more call that appears, on the surface of it, to be somewhat like that one, then let's examine the two calls, analyze the difference in them, and get into what people are actually saying with their words and actions.

I phoned Jimmy Bagwell, co-owner of Bagwell Elliott Auto Parts Co. in Charleston and said, "Jimmy, I'll be down to see you in a few hours. You going to be around?"

"Yes, Chuck. But if you are coming here to set up a

dealer meeting and program and sell me some barrels of shock absorbers, save your time. We're not going to run a program this year."

"O.K. But it is time to check your stock and update your catalogues, plus handle any inventory returns in your stock, so I'll see you in a few hours."

Much later, after the visit with Jimmy, Tommy Files, Jimmy's purchasing agent, told me a very funny story. He said Jimmy came into his office right after talking to me on the phone and said, "Tommy, Chuck Lewis is coming down here to sell us some barrels of shocks and set up a dealer meeting. I'm not going to hold a meeting and don't you give him an order for any barrels."

Tommy said Jimmy walked out but paused about six feet down the hall, his head cocked to one side reflectively. Then he slowly turned, re-entered the office and said, "Tommy, after Chuck has been here awhile I'm probably going to come back here and tell you to go ahead and give him an order for the barrels. If you do it, you're fired."

How about that for sales resistance? How would you like to walk into that situation? Of course, ignorance is bliss, and I didn't know about this when I walked in the door.

Jimmy hit me after I had handled all the service details of the sales call. Before I could say one word, he began. "Chuck, don't even get started on your sales pitch for barrels and a dealer meeting. Do you realize that we had to exchange shock absorbers with the dealers for a month after last year's program? The barrel contains shocks for Ford, Plymouth and Chevy and it seemed like all they sold were Buick, Pontiac and Nash. It drove us crazy making all those exchanges. And besides, the dealers seem to be getting a little too relaxed, like they don't want to bother with programs this year. We didn't get rich on the last one after making all those exchanges and the dealers are not receptive for another one. And I told you on the phone not to come down here looking for an order."

I looked at this fine man and had no words. I'd gotten out of the habit of begging. Now it was either reason or walk. I stood there empty, not knowing what to say. Then a wall display of civic awards, community membership plaques and sales awards caught my eye.

"Jimmy, you are probably right in everything you say. I can't argue with any of it. But the truth is that it is the responsibility of leaders of business to continue, even in the face of discouragement, to do everything you can to upgrade your dealers and your industry. You cannot, in good conscience, refuse to do your best with a sales program. How about our scheduling the meeting for the 15th of next month and work with your salesmen for three days after the meeting?"

Jimmy sighed, "O.K."

Now I only had one problem to solve. Tommy wouldn't give me a purchase order! I had to phone it instead of having it on paper.

Now, what is the difference between the sale to Jimmy Bagwell and the sale to the wise guy? On the surface of it I appealed to the pride of each man and they sold themselves based on their own conception of themselves.

The difference is in the quality of the pride each man possessed and the way they used it. The wise guy was using false pride as a crutch, trying to prop himself up with a peacock strut. Jimmy had some pride too, but it was a perfectly harmless element for both of us.

Pride is one of two things. It can be a static unmoving self-concept that becomes a rigid position. When pride is utilized this way then people will do just about anything to defend their position.

The other way, pride is simply a dedication to moving forward toward excellence, a search for quality. It isn't static, and doesn't have a rigid position to defend.

The arrogant proud man purchased because I placed his pride right on the line. His only other alternative would have been to take a swing at me. He didn't look like a hitter, just a talker, so I gave him a choice that had only one way out of it. Buy the program. There was a third choice, but it was too tough. He could have discarded his pride, then made his decision based on how the deal looked from a lot of other angles.

In contrast, Jimmy purchased simply to help his dealers remain strong. He wasn't out to defend or prove anything.

But there is also a difference in how those two sales felt inside me. Sure, I got an order from the wise guy. But to do it, I became like him. I walked out of his door proud. Then guess what? On the next call I thought I could whip the world again. No sale.

But coming away with an order from Jimmy Bagwell carried nothing but satisfaction for both of us. Jimmy ran the program and we enjoyed each other's company for several more years before my job change carried me out of his industry. He is a fine man of good purpose.

We started out discussing fear and it ended up as a discussion of pride. Off the subject? No. Fear and pride are identically the same thing.

When it doesn't have any fear in it, pride is not pride at all. It is simply a dedication to excellence.

CHAPTER 3

Lawyers and Judges, Eskimos and Super Salesmen

When I learned to listen to other people and actually hear what they were saying, not only with their words, but also with their whole outlook on life, I began to fully understand that it is always the customer who buys, never the salesman selling. Many people do not believe this, particularly salesmen. Many salesmen go out to "Knock 'em dead."

It is a paradox. The greatest compliment many people can think of for a salesman is, "He could sell iceboxes to Eskimos!" Perhaps. But purchase orders often are transformed into a tangible recognition symbol of self-worth. In this way, an insecure super salesman who found himself stuck in the arctic with nothing but iceboxes, Eskimos, and time on his hands would hustle to find some way of proving himself, or more accurately, to avoid being a bum in his own self-perception. No one else would consider him a bum, just himself.

The main point in this is that when a salesman focuses on his own fears, or without even focusing on it, just blindly assumes he must go out to seek conquest of his challenge, he often sees and perceives the customer as being the source of his difficulty. The customers are "tough." I've got to bear down on this one. He is about to get away from me. The customer becomes the challenge. So the salesman decides to operate on an adversary system. The customer resists. The salesman persists. Wear them down, overpower them with logic. Defeat their objections. Prove it so a six-year-old can see it plainly, and just incidentally, without really intending to, make the prospect feel like he is six years old as the conversation proceeds. No sale. Or a sale that contains no real satisfaction for the salesman as he keeps his fingers crossed hoping the buyer will not cancel later. Then there is the other fear. All that logic and all that persuasion painted a totally rosy picture for the buyer. When the goods are actually delivered, will that rosy glow become a reality? Or will it simply be remembered as one more promise from a too enthusiastic salesman?

Selling this way places the buyer in the position of a judge, the salesman as a defendant, or it places them in an adversary position as opposing lawyers. In either case it creates a relationship that contains battle or pleas. The feeling the salesman has later is one of either luck or power. Yet in reviewing the sale process the big ingredient is often overlooked. Whether it was pleas or power that "won," it was in reality the buyer's decision that determined the outcome.

Another danger of power selling with personal concepts of an adversary system is that later, if the salesman has social conscience, he may feel awed by the power he now believes he possesses.

In this way, a quest for sales which was born in the salesman's emotional need to go out on the street to prove himself now advances to the position of simply proving to the salesman that all he proved was that he overpowered another human being and maybe hurt someone in the process. Now we have two negatives plaguing the emotions of the salesman: his original self-doubt and his new regret of power. Many people either quit selling at this point or dislike themselves more every day. And still, in all of this the salesman conceives himself as the source of power. The feeling is, I've got power to persuade and I'm doing battle with it. Sometimes this appraisal is totally correct. Right here, the big question might be, "Did my product soothe and eliminate some fear the prospect already possessed, or did I inject a lot of needless fear into him to make him want my product? Did I enlighten the prospect about some unseen future problem that actually exists in his pathway, or did I deliberately throw some stumbling blocks into this person's life?"

All selling begins with a product, or an objective. If there is nothing you wish to have another person do, of what purpose is selling? Because this is true a person can form a plus or minus personal outlook on the projected effort to receive agreement. What is the value of a "yes" if it leads out to a worthless result or a result that is as harmful as helpful? And though this is true, and even after selecting the finest product with the maximum good benefit, it is still possible to conceive prospects as judges.

We are, all of us, mirrors of each other. When we believe we see someone judging us it is usually because we first have judged ourselves. We judge ourselves first as without worth, then decide to do something of value, believing this gives us worth. Now, in order for this to succeed, the people we deal with must go along with our plan. If they fail to do so their action is a vote that says "No worth." So in this way we look for our worth in other people. They become a mirror for us to look into to approve of ourselves. Because we do not wish to appear without worth, we do everything we can to get the other person to agree.

This can get twisted around into the adversary or judge system approach. The unspoken emotional dialogue becomes: "I say I am of worth, and you may wish to resist reaffirming this. You may not agree. We will struggle with this until one of us convinces the other. And since I am the instigator of the struggle I will overpower you if I can, not because I do not like you, but because I must. My worth is on the line. Therefore, before I go out the door to come see you, I'll look in my glass mirror, wink at myself, smile, and say, 'I'm going to knock 'em dead,' or, 'They are going to love me today.' When I finally arrive to see you, my real life mirror, my comment becomes, 'You're gonna love it!' In this mood, when I speak to present my idea to you I am pleading with you to see it so as to help me agree on my worth, and if you refuse, I will state my own logic about this idea to you with even greater conviction. The risk is if I give up my idea I also give up my self-worth."

Now, what is the logic or emotional appeal of this proposal to the other person? How do they benefit by helping the salesman achieve his self-worth if to do so they must agree with a proposal using the salesman's reasons and logic?

The answer, of course, is that there is no value at all to the buyer to reach agreement using a consideration of benefit that will apply to any other person except himself. The buyer is there to seek his benefit, not the benefit of the salesman. The benefit to the salesman is commission, not self-approval.

Because this is true, all power moves or weak supplications from the salesman simply get in the way of the buyer's mental and emotional outlook toward the product. In selling the focus should be upon the buyer, not the salesman. The single question the buyer has for the salesman whether spoken or not, is, "What's in it for me?"

The goal is simply to become more adept at presenting benefits to the buyer so thoroughly that the buyer wants to purchase. When this goal is accomplished there is no purpose served by either power or pleading. The challenge becomes one of being able to investigate the prospect's needs and desires. In all of this, because the focus is on the prospect, the salesman is neutral and not threatened emotionally by the outcome.

The buyer's power is a real and constant determiner of agreement, but the buyer is often diverted from acting as a buyer by incorrect selling attitudes. If a salesman attempts to overpower the buyer, the buyer must use his power or energy in repelling the strident press he feels and experiences as a threat. For every action there is a reaction.

When the seller places the buyer in position as a judge, the buyer will still react, but instead of just pushing the sales appeal away the buyer now will respond by doing exactly what he was asked to do: judge. The buyer will play a destructive judging game with the seller. In this relationship of judge and plaintiff the seller often is ahead of the game when the buyer refuses to purchase, because if the buyer has a firm hand as judge he will extract so many concessions from the seller that all the profit in the transaction disappears in escalated costs to the seller, either in dollars or in emotions.

The focus must be neutral, neither upon the force nor weakness of the salesman, but rather upon the benefits of agreement. True, buyers often give orders to a salesman simply because the salesman is enjoyed as a personal contact, and all selling of this type begins with simple friendship. Friendship selling will gain much business, but never any more than the buyer intended to give. To influence the buyer to reach for a larger concept there also must be a pleasant yet persistent confrontation of the inertia the buyer is experiencing. The confrontation is directed toward the inertia, not the buyer.

It is one matter to have a salesman deliver a commodity regularly to a chain of stores and quite another matter to send a salesman to those same stores to sell the owners on the idea of opening a brand new untried department within the store.

My grandfather, not the one on the vegetable truck, the other grandfather, was widely known throughout the South as "Opening Bill" Lewis. This nickname derived from his skill in traveling to small towns, finding and forming friendships with the local people of money and inducing them to open a ten cent store in the town. After bringing his prospect to Atlanta to select the inventory, while being boarded and entertained by "Opening Bill" and my grandmother, the opening bill of goods, the beginning inventory for the new store, was shipped. Then a regular route salesman was assigned to the account and "Opening Bill" Lewis studied the railroad time table to pick his next town, finding his most enjoyable challenge in an approach to totally unknown people in unseen towns, discussing a totally new venture.

In either type selling, either as route salesman or as "Opening Bill," there is first acceptance by the prospect. Call it acceptance or call it friendship, either way the salesman has two objectives. One, to be liked, but more, to have his idea liked. The error in power or plea selling is that most of the focus is upon the salesman and little upon the product. The reason this approach fails is that the value lies in the benefits of the product, not in the declaration of the worth of the salesman.

The simple question in appraising a salesman is not,

"Can he sell?" or, "Is he a regular fellow?" but rather is, "Do his customers benefit from his services and products?" Because this is true the salesman can relax and let go of his fear of being of little worth. It is only an insecure salesman who can "sell iceboxes to Eskimos."

Now how does a salesman articulate all of this internally and put it into practice daily as he meets his prospects? Very simple. He focuses upon the benefits his prospect will receive from the product and then pretends to actually be the prospect so he can figure out if the benefits are worth the price paid. Then he pretends to be the prospect again as he faces the prospect. To state this plainly, the salesman becomes the exact person his prospect is in order to see the product from the correct emotional considerations. If the prospect is proud the salesman must pretend and say, "I am proud. Now how does this proposal fit in with my pride?" or, "I want some advantage. What advantage is there in this product for me?"

As the salesman pretends to be the buyer the concern for acceptance as either a power force or a nice guy is replaced with a new concern for the buyer. When the salesman does this successfully he listens to his own words to discover how they sound to this other new part of him, the buyer. In this way the salesman is both buyer and seller in his own mind.

Now suppose the real prospect does not purchase. What does the salesman do next, shoot himself to at least eliminate that part of the buyer?

If agreements are elusive, the salesman must study his craft thoroughly to discover how he may improve. Generally, the first area of improvement is to turn loose of all concepts of self-worth based upon performance and concentrate instead upon the potential agreements that can

45

be reached by improving the selling attitudes and methods. It is just a learning process, not a field of honorable combat. In every situation everyone wins. There are no losers. Each person walks away with a lesson.

Some salesmen use a term, "lost sale." A salesman may say, "I lost the sale." Really? How long was it owned? Where was it purchased? Was it one of your favorite sales or just one you picked up and don't really care for very much? Was it insured? Where had you been storing it before you "lost" it?

There is no such thing as a "lost sale," because there never have been any "sales owned." There are only sales made and sales that the salesman didn't quite make and like all unfinished things, if it is examined carefully perhaps a reason for the slow-down in the scheme of things can be discovered. When this happens the discovery so made is now a lesson learned. Viewed in this perspective can the salesman not lighten up on his harsh judgment of himself?

To accomplish this all ego must be released and in the place of pride a dedication to excellence in study must be used. There is only one way to actually be a failure. It is to refuse to learn. As long as the salesman learns, each small lesson is a success. There are no lost sales. There are only lessons learned and improvement achieved.

These are the questions that produce learning and growth. The salesman should ask them alone after the encounter with the prospect has ended:

> What was the prospect's need? How could he benefit from possession of the product or acceptance of the service?

> What was the prospect's attitude? Beneath this attitude, what was his emotional outlook? What was he feeling?

Did I explain the product or service in such a way as to achieve maximum harmony with the prospect's emotions? Did I tailor my remarks to fit the exact way this prospect operates emotionally? If not, how, specifically, did I miss? What element of the prospect's emotions was not soothed or motivated?

Why did I receive a refusal intead of an agreement? What was the prospect's main reason for refusal? I know I am a person of worth and some ability, so this next answer does not defeat me emotionally, but still, did I act in some negative way? Did I act in a positive way and yet still not blend in well with the prospect's attitude?

How could I have done this more effectively?

Is it too late? Can I go back again to correct an oversight? Can I present a further idea or motivation? How? When? Why do I believe a second effort will achieve agreement?

If I make a second approach, am I not learning by applying the wisdom of my reflections?

Because I didn't "lose" the sale, am I not simply working to achieve it? And if this second try does not gain agreement can I not learn yet another lesson and improve still more?

Isn't all this simply a sale that isn't quite completed yet?

What on earth am I doing to myself if I allow my ego to control the answers to any of these questions or control my next action?

Is there possibly a "lost me" involved here instead of the "lost sale"? Isn't that what I've done, let my ego tell me I am the sale and then when I believe I have a "lost sale" then I also have a "lost me"? Isn't this somewhat ridiculous to consider myself in these negative erroneous terms?

What is my next positive move to achieve agreement?

In reflecting on the above questions consider this as the definition of selling. The sole function of the salesman is to hold up, in plain view, exactly what the prospect desires in order that it may be purchased. The sole task facing the salesman is to discover what it is that the prospect desires. What the prospect desires is never the actual product or even the benefits produced by the product but rather the emotional satisfaction produced by the benefits. In a relationship with any other person the appeal is to the emotions. There is no such substance as logic. Take any bit of supposed logic, dissect it, and you will discover an emotion that created the logic.

The key question is not "how?" It is "why?"

CHAPTER 4

Patients and Patience

In the grip of fear people snatch any hope of salvation, leading to much prayer in foxholes under bombardment and in planes when an engine fails, relative in direct proportion to the number of working engines remaining or the density of the bombardment. Sellers often bombard buyers with potential dangers magnified beyond all reasonable level of probability, and in this atmosphere fear-motivated buyers often purchase unwanted products. But battles end, planes land and sellers exit. Later, the frantic grasp for salvation becomes a quiet reflection, and while some continue attending church others just send the product back and stop payment on their check.

All fear is simply the reverse of desire. Sellers of desire help buyers make the journey to the other side of the issue.

Desire creates potential reality to work toward rather than escape from as it is with fear. Fear can be escaped after an anxious moment but desires tantalize forever and even when achieved lead to further desire. Thus a seller of fear becomes a victim of his product as he dreads the changing mind of his buyer, while those who sell desire look forward to the buyer's additional thoughts.

Fear can always, except in actual dire emergencies, be transposed into awareness and a commitment to excellence. When a child is told never to touch a stove, is that fear-inducing? No, it is simply awareness. The same stove that can burn is also a tool to use in producing apple pie. Is the child supposed to fear apple pie because it came out of the stove, or just be aware that it needs to cool a bit before eating it?

Actually, even in emergencies, fear isn't the answer either. Awareness of an escape route coupled with a desire for survival is the only hope of salvation.

The urge to survive is the natural human condition. This urge is merely a dedication to excellence. Isn't life itself the basic excellence? Only when people become confused in their thinking does fear become the habitual condition. You know someone like this, someone who always sees the danger in everything and spends most of their time huddled up protectively hoping to avoid disaster, or discomfort, or inconvenience, or expense, or hurt emotions, or disease or a thousand other vague threats.

The key ingredient in persuading people is to help them focus upon their desires instead of their fears. The first stage is to treat a hazard with awareness, then add in a search for excellence.

But people are complex. Fear often causes people to react aggressively. Instead of huddling in a protective posture, many people react with a form of anger. When this happens a direct assault upon the imagined fear element is launched. If you are perceived by this person as a threat of any kind you will be resisted. When you are perceived as a soothing element you will be accepted.

All of this happens in a large scale of increasing or decreasing intensity. Psychiatrists use the term "lethality" to grade the seriousness of a problem emotion. How lethal is it? If a patient dislikes someone, which really means just that he fears being able to relate well to them, the question is, what is he most likely to do about it? The answer reveals the lethality in the situation. Once the degree of lethality is known a treatment can begin. For a few this means hospitalization. For others, verbal therapy. This is always a puzzle, this fear business.

A person fears being able to relate well to someone. So why try? Why not just walk away when it is too hard to relate? Because our natural condition is the urge to join with others.

In everyday life we all are each other's patients and each other's doctors. What is selling, or more simply, persuading, other than doctoring a situation and offering people a cure? And just as a doctor must rate the existing degree of lethality, so must we as persuaders.

During a short stint selling brass fittings in the automotive trade, I entered a garage carrying a small cabinet which I intended to sell to the prospect for stocking brass fittings. He took one look at the fittings box, turned red in the face, and stated in a deadly, soft voice, "If that is a brass fitting case you have there, I will give you exactly to the count of three to get out. If you are still here when I'm through I'm going to beat the living hell out of you."

Guess which way I started moving? But as I backpedaled to the door I said, "I don't blame you for being angry, but I know why you're mad. One of my competitors came through here last month and overloaded everybody. How much did he stick you with?"

The man turned to a cabinet, jerked the door open and said, "Come see for yourself."

Why can't I keep my big mouth shut? He wants me to come closer. I hesitated. I had him figured as a hitter. His face softened just a little after he saw my hesitation. Finally, quiet and meek as Mary's little lamb I walked over to his cabinet and looked. With fittings, few customers really understand all the variety of items. So they trust a salesman to write the order fairly. This man's trust had been abused. He was overloaded.

"It makes me mad, too. You are very overstocked. Now you are mad at all fittings salesmen. Look, I can't make it up to you for what someone else did, but I can show you how to avoid this kind of trickery in the future."

"Yeah? How?"

"No problem. My company packages the fittings just five to a bag. When you run low, just order one bag. The other difficult thing, you know, identifying the fittings, is also made simple. You don't have to trust anybody by signing an order you don't understand because this cabinet has a picture of each fitting on the individual drawer fronts and the part number is right there under the picture. See? You can write your own order. If you like this idea, I'll sort all your fittings into this cabinet and you can become a customer. If you need any item today it will be just a small bag of five you get. You will have to write the order for me. What do you say?"

He thought about it and said, "O.K. But if you overload me . . ."

"You've already made the consequences clear and, believe me, I believe you. But anyway, you will have to help me write the order by looking at the pictures." I changed his stock over and he ordered a few items he needed, then later, reordered from my local jobber.

This man was lethal to the extreme degree. Very honestly, if there hadn't been a sales counter between us when he first spoke I don't know if I would have tried any response at all.

Please take a moment to consider the three layers of negatives in the man. First, anger at a past situation, soothed by my backing away. All anger is in reality fear, and he feared a repeat wound. Second, a suspicion of me in his future. This suspicion disappeared as I became his ally, becoming angry with him at the previous injury. Third, the simple doubt about the product, a harmless element in itself. Doubt is merely the step preceding knowledge and acceptance. My explanation of my product removed this doubt, allowing him to trust. Always look for the separate specific elements in people's anger. First, neutralize the anger, then deal with the suspicion by creating trust as an ally, then proceed to create belief with factual helpful information which dissolves the doubt. It has to happen one step at a time. Did I know all that when it was happening? Of course not! Later in the book we will look at an inner computer we all possess which allows us to feel our way through such situations even when we have no articulate knowledge of just what is happening.

But most people are not lethal to that degree. So instead of a definite threat, the encounter produces a verbal, "I'm busy," or, "We don't need anything today," or even a lie, "I'm broke." With people who consider themselves to be very fair, sometimes they will let you give a sales presentation, then politely say, "No." Sometimes the "no" is their way of expressing a hostility as much as stating they do not desire the product. Others, having forgiven the other salesmen from the past, just say "no" without any other external factor present in them except the single statement that they do not want any product today.

So how can a sale be made? It looks too complex, doesn't it? The objective is to sell without harm. But when a "no" is received is it for real or is it just an expression of some fear? How can you tell the difference? Surely you don't want to push in on someone if they have no real use for the product. But on the other hand, if the "no" sent me away it is also a loss for the customer. I'm gone, and the next salesman may be another overloader type. So the prospect keeps sending salemen away until one day he is out of product and must trust someone again. Looks to me like he is in danger again. Now, if I have a way to help him protect himself, haven't I done him a disservice if I let him dismiss me too quickly? Some say, "That's his problem." This is a very private, individual decision each person must make. For me, I get a kick out of it when I can see a person calm down and accept me and help me form some kind of harmony. Maybe it just proves I either need or like people, maybe a strange mixture of both. Maybe I cannot function totally alone. I'd probably make a poor hermit. How about you?

CHAPTER 5

You're Gonna Love It

With all these varying levels of fear, suspicion, and doubt between people in selling situations, how can anyone ever sell or, stated more accurately, assist prospects in purchasing?

Let's approach the question slowly. If those negatives are the blockages in the sale, and if we want to dissolve those blockages, in which direction are we heading? What single word defines the exact opposite of fear? And if we know this word, can we accept it as the natural direction of all efforts?

The word we are searching for is love. It sounds too simple, doesn't it? O.K. Let's try for another word if you prefer. How about that last word—prefer? or like? or desire? or trust? All these words are only a softer, watered down expression of the word love.

Sometimes salesmen, in a burst of enthusiasm, exclaim, "You're gonna love it!" Isn't this what we are aiming for, to present something the other person is going to love? Can we not say that all of our less intense words such as prefer and like and trust are simply words that mean love?

So when we assist someone in avoiding or eliminating a fear, haven't we assisted them toward love? It is routine for the woman to kiss the fireman who saves her child. It is usual for a big smile to be exchanged for a sudden favor that prevents loss. Even if someone you think you do not like should say, "Here, you dropped this twenty dollar bill," and held it out for you, your natural reaction would be to say, "Thank you." As you do, you also lose some of the distrust of that person. If you are not careful, and if that person does half a dozen other nice acts which benefit you, you will find yourself liking them.

All of this being true, do I have your permission to not only use the word love but also examine it in detail as we have been examining the word fear?

In any negotiating situation the first goal is to dissolve all doubt, suspicion, and anger. All of those elements are simply fear. We wish to dissolve fear because when we do the next substance we find is love.

When a customer expresses, or simply displays, fear of me, there is only one of two sources for the fear.

First, someone from their past may have done them some disservice, injury, slight, economic damage, physical damage, or mental intimidation. Or, the person may have caused themselves harm by making a decision that didn't work out too well for them. When fear is of the past it may be specific. Some incident is remembered and now this transaction we are engaging in today reminds them of this past event. Or I remind them of that person from the past and I become a feared person.

Second, the fear may be of some unseen event in the future, perhaps a real scheduled event, or even a dreaded nameless expectation that some unidentified occurrence may become harmful in some way. If I am perceived as a bearer or instigator of this future event I will be feared.

Very seldom is a fear an expression of what is actually happening this exact moment. Even if one person were pointing a gun at someone, the fear is of the pain that will be inflicted if and when the trigger is pulled. All that exists in the exact present is awareness of a reality being experienced. The fear is of the next moment and what it will bring. The fear is real in the present but it focuses upon the dreaded future event which may occur.

Few people are totally successful in always performing in the exact present moment. When this does happen a calm exists in the person that is easily noticed by any nearby person.

Think about this a moment to perceive it fully in your own personal emotional experience. Forget yesterday. Forget tomorrow. All that is left is today. Not even today, just this exact moment, one split second. There is a blank, filled only by what is occurring this precise second. Now focus upon some beautiful object. Simply absorb its beauty and tranquility. A special time may be needed to do this act of neutral observation. Yet each of us has those moments. Perhaps it is a few moments when the eyes are first opened on a lazy weekend morning. Nothing has just happened except sleep, in which there were no unpleasant dreams. You have not yet focused on the beginning of any activity which will start your day. You have gently awakened from sleep. The night has ended and the day has not begun. There is no thought, but instead the gaze sees only a ray of sun on the wall or pillow. The mind is a complete blank, not captivated by thought. Instead, there is a visual perception only of what the eyes open to see. None of it really registers yet. There is a gentleness in this and a total absence of fear, for no past or future exists in this one brief moment.

A voice is heard.

"Honey, do you want waffles or bagels?"

Oops! There went that moment. Let me see now, I'm trying to lose weight. I wonder if the waffles will taste alright without very much syrup. The last time I ate a bagel I got heartburn. I wonder why we can't have eggs?

"Honey, which do you want?"

"I'm thinking about it."

Now, if the voice is a minor disruption of the totally empty peace of the moment and waffles a challenge, how about a meeting with a prospect?

If a waffle or a bagel can produce concern, how about an impending soon-to-occur proposition about agreeing on something unknown at this first moment of contact? And it isn't just the food item, it is also a concern to reply to the other person in a pleasant way. Otherwise there is some anxiety formed in everyone. Most people really want to respond to a new arrival in a pleasant way even when the arrival is a salesman.

What follows may seem out of place in a book about selling. It needs to be diluted to the level of acceptable social moves appropriate to the exact situation being experienced.

The best way to start the day off right with the mate is to have a hug and a soft word. The love expressed gets rid of any anxiety about the waffles for a moment and any hesitant pause to see how they are going to relate this morning.

In the interaction of a sales situation, if the salesperson reaches out to hug Sam and the salesperson's name is Pete and both are heterosexual, a good bit of confusion is going to spring up that promotes fear instead of abolishing it. So instead we smile and shake hands, and when the eyes smile it means even more than when the mouth does the job alone. The only element missing in love which is expressed as friendship is the sexual element.

A salesman must love people. Some people expect a salesman to always like to go to ball games and crowded parties as evidence of loving people. But when the hug is given to the mate it is to one person, and a salesman can stay out of crowds all his life and still express love for people. It only counts one person at a time anyway.

One truth stands above all else. Love is to be experienced and considered in a very personal way. No concept or book can carry a person through the experience intellectually. It has to be felt and experienced.

The following words are simply one concept of love. This concept is one of action, not idle definition, and particularly, a concept totally related to one person influencing another. There are other concepts of love such as the static pleasure of an experience which has no objective in mind, such as visiting in a home and saying, "I like that painting," knowing full well there is not present also a desire to personally own it.

Love means knowledge of the other person, some awareness of who they are, how they function, where they come from, where they are going, and how they are feeling at this exact moment.

Acceptance, another of love's characteristics, means a very neutral opinion of the person being loved, an absence of judging, a refusal to assign negatives to either what they are or how they are acting or where they say they are heading.

Concern means simply the feeling that "it matters." It matters that here is a human being, in some ways like yourself, who is someone you know and accept. This person has hopes and aspirations and also some problems to solve or old misconceptions to overcome as he progresses in life.

Commitment means simply that you pledge yourself to the other person's overall welfare. You can put yourself in his shoes for a moment, think about his trip in a very personal way, and make a private, silent agreement to assist him. It matters to you how he is able to proceed and you determine to assist him in his trip in a way that does not harm either of you.

Finally, all of this is possible only when you release all of your own fears related to this encounter. You have knowledge of the other person, accept him as he is, and have become concerned about him. You accept him with neutrality, refusing to judge him. In all of this he may have fears. Sometimes in selling one of the simplest fears is that the time spent with a salesman is wasted. A more complex fear is that the salesman will persuade and influence until an unwanted product is puchased. These are two very real fears. It is not the prospect's job to release these fears in himself. It is the salesman's commitment to accept the prospect with all his fears and at the same time to act with concern. To do so the salesman must release his own fears.

Now, how does the salesman let go of his own fears? The rules of the game are equal. The salesman, to let go of fear, must proceed toward loving himself as surely as he loves people. These rules of love are the same, whether directed toward others or self. To love yourself, use the same four concepts used in expressing love for other people: Knowledge of self, acceptance of self, concern for your well-being, and commitment to finding your own truths.

To mix with other people with love, add in these ingredients. Know that all persons are alike in more ways than they are different and you are like all people. Accept this universal brotherhood. Be concerned for the involvement with this person to whom you are relating and be equally concerned about yourself. Commit to the simple desire to achieve mutual beneficial harmony and form agreement.

In all of this, the following actions and thoughts will ensure success:

Forget yesterday. It is gone.

Do not focus on tomorrow. It hasn't arrived.

Accept the present as the only time that exists.

Do not judge yourself or other people.

Be neutral.

Figure out what is happening right now and relate to that alone.

Relate to other people as they indicate their present needs and desires.

When these seven points are observed and followed, the ego is stilled and fear is released. No misconception of fear from the past can govern the transaction of this instant. No dread or narrow plan relating to the future can govern this instant. Only what is happening at this instant can govern this instant.

At first, this focus upon this instant seems to be, perhaps, a mindless vacuum, a state of no purpose, a neutrality without any forward movement. Yet there is no true, exact rest. Everything moves forward of its own accord. Everyone's heart beats. The lungs inhale and exhale. The world turns. The day progresses.

When you look at another person for two seconds, they move in some direction or another, either smile to advance the meeting, frown to slow it down, or remain strangely neutral, which tells you it may be your turn to make a move. When you speak to say hello, your action creates a reaction in them. It all flows.

Let it flow. Do not be afraid of this action, the movement. Do not attempt to control it, but rather seek to observe how the interaction proceeds. You are part of the action, and the other person is also an equal part of the action. Allow each of you the freedom to move in any direction that feels right.

Now, with this relaxed peace and in the presence of the other person, all new movement and all new action is experienced as a flow as you allow yourselves to form a harmony.

When the other person is angry when you arrive, allow yourself to know that you are not responsible for their anger, and do not fear it, but simply be aware that you wish to dissolve it so it does not hurt you or the other person. Anger usually hurts the one who has it as much as the person who receives it, so your love for others tells you to do nothing which will increase the anger and anything which will reduce it and eliminate it. You know you have not made any absolute plan for how the other person is going to feel or how you are going to feel, and so you know you are free to move in a more favorable direction. Equally important, by not believing the other person's anger is absolute, or an unchangeable fact, you give them permission to change, to move, to proceed toward peace. There is neutrality in this feeling, and peace.

CHAPTER 6

Doubt, Trust, Observation and Truth

When I left the shock absorber business I took a job as a sales engineer in the hydraulic hose business. The Aeroquip Corporation hired me in their personnel department, in Jackson, Michigan, then assigned me, sight unseen, to work as a salesman with Bill Pritchett, a fine man and the district sales manager for the southeastern states.

Bill is a rugged war hero who earned captain's bars in combat for his bravery and leadership. You may have heard of the daring raid on a supposedly impenetrable German fortification in a castle situated high on a mountain in Italy. Bill was in a team of commandos who scaled that mountain face, hand over hand on climbing ropes, to attack by surprise and seize the castle. If you ask Bill to do 50 pushups he would grin and ask, "With which hand?" He also is as friendly as Santa Claus, except he doesn't give anything away. You have to earn it with Bill.

The company carved out a territory for me by giving me the tag ends of three other salesmen's territories. From Lew Ely I obtained southern Georgia, from Arnie Lane the extreme north section of Florida, and from Jerry Holcomb the entire state of South Carolina.

When Bill and I sat down to discuss the accounts, he reviewed his impressions of each customer. Then I was further familiarized with the accounts by the former salesmen in the territory who escorted me around to shake hands with the customers.

Jerry Holcomb is somewhat similar to Bill. Jerry marched out of the infamous Chosin Reservoir as a marine in the Korean conflict. Another fine man with a devilish, pleasant humor, but tough as a hickory nut under the surface.

One account in particular became a focal point for me in the territory. The Cline Company in Greenville, South Carolina had purchased $12,000 per year from the company for a period of ten years. This volume of business was extraordinarily low. As a comparison, another account had been purchasing at the $75,000 level.

Bill and Jerry were unanimous in their appraisal of Cline Company. "They buy a little from us. But we can never go big with them because they are not loyal to us. Every competitor we have has their products on Cline's shelf. We have offered to get to work with them in earnest if they will stock just our line, but they refuse to throw those other lines out. We have protested time and again but they refuse to be loyal to us. Don't waste your time with them. Call on them two or three times a year to give them service but look for another distributor in their area."

Mr. N. Q. Cline, Sr., is somewhat deceptive. In contrast to Bill's dark navy suit and dark tie and Jerry's colorful sport jacket, Mr. Cline dresses in pale blue sport jacket and jaunty bow tie. While Bill and Jerry speak with great strength tempered into a statement of purpose, Mr. Cline speaks so softly at times that you must lean forward to hear him. Yet he is as resolved as either Bill or Jerry, and listens only to his own truths. A former sales supervisor for Sears, he one day tired of bigness and began selling oil from his home garage, transferring later to a small store.

He gradually added four more products to his line of oil, enlarged his store, and while he did an exactingly perfect job of giving his customers everything and anything they wanted in those five service product lines, he had little interest in becoming a typical big distributor handling 100 different products. Resisting bigness, he concentrated on thoroughness. Each of his employees was a specialist, for not only did he limit his products, he also assigned men to work with mainly one product, helping out other men only as the total business flow demanded.

Coming into this scene, I felt like a wet sock in a clothes dryer. Fresh from Aeroquip's ninety day product school, totally inexperienced in industrial sales, I began getting the heat from everyone as I was tossed around between several buffeting rigid positions. In addition to the disappointment for Cline Company felt by Jerry and Bill, Mr. Cline immediately conveyed his very softly stated displeasure with the demands and protests of Aeroquip Corporation. It was in his mood more than his words.

When people state differing views in a challenging way the antagonism permeates the air, clouding the entire interaction. Cline's employees picked up their mood from everyone—N. Q. Cline, Sr., Bill and Jerry. Mr. Cline had softly resisted the advances and protests of Bill and Jerry and his employees acted exactly the same way, for the employees had been selected for their loyalty as much as their working skills. As the new salesman I received the same resistance.

After Jerry completed his week with me making the introductory rounds of the territory, I returned to Cline Company for another visit. The employees were cool and reserved in one way, as a rejection of the formal position my company had established in trying to tell them how to run their business. But that was O.K. because I was confused and it didn't matter because I didn't know what to say next with them. But I was curious.

It's funny. We watch a Sherlock Holmes movie and assume the sleuthing is some nearly supernatural process, some keen intellect hot on the trail of a lesser mortal, smelling the air, testing the firmness of the soil, peering intently, sniffing everywhere, looking under and behind bushes. The whole thing seems to have an instinct about it in the same way a good bird dog sniffs out a covey of quail. Then Sherlock reassures his amazed helper by saying, "Elementary, Watson." And we sit there and silently believe it is elementary only for so keen an intellect as the great Sherlock. The movie ends, we go home, and if we are not careful we let all manner of clues go by us as we try to figure things out in our own mysteries. After all, we are just mortals, not the great Sherlock. Nuts.

In Cline's store, there was a puzzle. On a prominent front shelf I had noticed some very special hydraulic hose fittings manufactured by my company. Most fittings are fairly commonplace, but these were special, the type very few people used. I hadn't seen any of them as I toured around meeting the other distributors and looking over their business and inventory. I asked one of the Cline countermen, "What do you have these in stock for? Some special customer?" "No. But someone may have a need for them. We try to stock everything the customer needs." As I digested that fact and poked around in their store talking with their employees, I kept getting this same mood from them. "We have what the customer needs even if it is an oddball item." After awhile a pick-up truck pulled into the parking lot. The sign on its door stated the name of a construction company located in a town east of Charlotte, North Carolina. Extracting one worn, burst hydraulic hose line, the driver brought it into the store and gave it to a counterman. As the driver settled in for a wait for the hose to be replaced, I asked him, "How far did you drive to get here?"

"From Aberlmarle."

That was beyond Charlotte and Charlotte was about a two hour drive on the freeway. I pursued it. "Is this the only reason for your trip to Greenville?"

"Yes."

Now here, I needed the help of Sherlock. Charlotte had three distributors for that same product. Why did this man drive right past those stores? On the surface of it, it seemed insane or at least wasteful of time and money.

"Well, it's a good day for a drive, isn't it?"

"No, not really. That truck bounces too much and the alignment is out on it. But our bulldozer is down with only a week left to finish the job. I need to get the hose line back, quick." Then he hesitated. He could see my mind working. He added, "It's easier to just drive on down here to Cline than to stop in Charlotte. Those distributors do not have the complete stock like Cline does. By the time I look all over Charlotte for the right parts, I can get here and get the part quicker. It saves a lot of time to just come here first for some things."

He could have added, "Elementary, Watson!" because his superior knowledge had just educated me.

After absorbing that, I went back to the shop where Gene DeHart and Charlie Painter were making up the man's hose line. They both looked up when I entered, then went back to their work without a word, quickly completing the job. After the hose had been taken back to the driver, I hung around in the shop. Gene and Charlie were a little cool at first. I started to speak to break the ice. One of them, I forget who, said, "I hope you are not going to give us a lot of talk about using your hose." How about that for being up front?

"No. But if you don't mind, I'd like to watch. I've just gotten out of the factory training school, and you know how schools are. You have to watch how it is done out in the field before you really get the hang of it."

This seemed to relax them. Charlie and Gene became instant teachers, volunteering information on easy ways to handle the hose and fittings, answering my questions, and generally becoming friendly. They seemed to get a kick out of telling it the way it was to a factory "expert" instead of hearing how it ought to be in someone else's definition. Over a period of a few visits we became friends. When a coffee break came we talked about personal things. Gene is a radio buff and talked about conversations he had with people in far off places. Charlie was deep into his family and church. There was a lot to talk about and they were very congenial.

While I was back in the shop I picked up a job ticket one day and asked, "How do you know which brand of hose to use?"

Gene said, "We use the one that does the best job. When any brand of hose will do the job as well as the next one, we just use the one we feel best about. Sometimes our salesmen specify the brand."

"Oh." Then I clammed up and watched some more.

Charlie broke the silence. "Look, we can use your hose. But we haven't used it in the past because your company has some funny notions about how we ought to run this shop."

"Yeah. I can appreciate that. Well, I appreciate any business at all that you give me." Then I clammed up again.

Slowly, they began reaching for my brand. When I saw

a completed hose line, or several, out on the counter, I went back to the shop and thanked them. They laughed it off. Both of them liked to kid. "Well, we don't want you to starve to death."

Meanwhile, these visits to Cline Company were being listed on my daily call sheet. Bill Pritchett phoned me, cheerful, voice booming, but still very hot on his concern about my activities. "Chuck, what on earth are you doing calling on the Cline Company so much? You better look around for a distributor who will be loyal to us."

Aeroquip had a policy that stated the salesman was the undisputed decision maker in his territory. I had the responsibility and the authority to select or cancel any distributors and to use my time in whatever direction I thought best. Still, Bill had some other supervisory responsibilities and I had to live with him. Hopefully in some harmony. Also, there is another point. "When you pick a fight with a giant, you don't quit when you're tired. You quit when he's tired." The giant in this instance was not just Bill Pritchett, a man whom I respected, but also the entire Aeroquip Company philosophy. Bill was merely echoing the company concern. I felt this company had reviewed my qualifications and decided to put me in a decision making position. Now I was alone with it. I also felt I could be through investigating and reach for the secret to Cline's business before I got into any seriously deep trouble with my company. Still, I was hesitant with Bill.

I made every excuse for my action instead of just coming straight out and telling Bill I believed Cline could become a winner. Then I went back to Cline for more visits.

"Neb" Cline, or N.Q. Cline, Jr., was young and eager to prove of value to the family business. Outgoing and competent, he was a perfect fit in his job as outside salesman. I began talking with him about selling our product. Like me, he was not totally familiar with the industrial market. But he was well accepted by his customers, as I was to find out.

Neb didn't actually realize that Cline Company possessed a big competitive edge on other hydraulic distributors. First, they were a specialty house and could concentrate on a few products. Second, by word of mouth, his company had already gained an advantage which was proven by the maintenance people coming so far in their service trucks for the products and service offered by Cline. Third, Cline's inventory was vastly superior to any other distributor in the Carolinas. Finally, if all this were presented to the purchasing agents there could be a flow of business greater than at present when it was mostly just the maintenance people who had such a high regard for the Cline service.

Neb and I began talking about a thorough effort to visit all the prospects in his area to tell the Aeroquip product story and the Cline service story. Neb listened to my ideas and thought about it. He, too, had been afflicted with the general pessimism directed toward Aeroquip because of the conflict over the subject of loyalty.

In all of this time, I never said a word to anyone at Cline Company about the loyalty question. When I saw my competitors' products being sold I kept my mouth shut. The way I had it figured, just part of Cline's business could be greater than 100 percent of another distributor's business. If you were told you could send someone into the Fort Knox gold depository and you could have all the gold they carried out in one trip, would you rather have what a weight lifter could carry out in one hand or what a six-year-old can carry out in two? Also, thanks to Gene and Charlie in the shop, my share of their existing business was already increasing.

The question hung in the air with Neb, whether to work hard with me or move in other directions. I continued to visit them at least two times a week. Finally one day he called me over to his desk.

"Chuck, you've been calling on us for six weeks. You've helped us, and you haven't made any strong demands. Everybody in this place likes you. You've never pressured us for an order. Today, I want you to mail this order in with your call report. Let them know you aren't coming here for nothing."

I looked at the order. It was a good one. Then I looked at Neb. He looked like he was either testing me or on the verge of something. I didn't know which one. Well, when in doubt, try to move forward.

I looked around at the windows. Sometimes, in the middle of something that makes sense I do something that doesn't make sense. Today I looked at the windows curiously.

Neb asked, "What are you looking for?"

"The sign."

"What sign?"

"The going-out-of-business sign. Neb, if you and I get down to work on the ideas we have been discussing, this order won't last until next Tuesday. Then we will be out of business."

"What's the matter with that order? I thought it was pretty good."

"No. Not if we are going to sell together, and I'm not overly concerned about impressing my boss by mailing in an order. If this is your idea of a good order I'll let you mail it in and wait for you to make up your mind about our plans. Then I'll mail in an order that reflects your commitment."

"I thought the order was a nice one."

"Sure it is, for a normal inventory restock. But you and I are talking about selling together with some real effort. If you want to do that, take your pen and double the quantities on that order."

This was his point of decision. He could go either way, toward the positives of our discussed plans, or shrug it off and look for another route to becoming of great value to his company.

He fished in his pocket for his pen and slowly doubled the order.

"O.K., buddy, but now I'm counting on you for some help."

"Get your list of customers ready for next Monday. My body and mind and sweat belongs to Cline Company for the entire week and any more time we need."

When we went together to sell as a team it developed that I could have stayed home. Neb told a very good story of his service and our product. Introducing me as the Aeroquip sales engineer, he said I could handle any hydraulic hose applications and solve any problems. Then when the customer gave us a look at their problems Neb solved them. He knew five brands of hose and fittings and could instantly relate someone else's product to the Aeroquip replacement. I grinned, twiddled my thumbs and watched him work. The best way to appear intelligent is to work with an even more intelligent person and let them do the talking.

The Cline volume, which had remained stagnant for ten years at $12,000 a year, rose to, if memory is correct, about $70,000 that first year. It never slowed down, eventually reaching $500,000 in one year.

Analysis of the "sale"

When I was first introduced to Cline Company, I doubted everything I was hearing, because it didn't agree with what I was seeing. Here was a distributor who was energetic and thorough and well-liked by the business community. Was I supposed to dislike them because of their "dis-loyalty"? I looked at the situation and believed they were totally loyal, but to their customers first, their suppliers second.

Now, was I supposed to dislike my company's stand? Aeroquip was, and still is, the undisputed quality leader in the hydraulic hose industry. Their sales policies are very fair and equitable. Being new, I didn't feel I could choose to dislike anything my company did.

But my trust was neither with Cline's distaste or Aeroquip's disappointment. These two factions had been in effect for ten years, producing no good result. The whole atmosphere was negative, not positive. Aeroquip gave me authority in my territory. O.K. Fair enough. If I am told I may decide, then get ready for me to be something other than a carbon copy of every previous decision. Following blindly is not deciding. Only carefully figuring things out is a deciding process.

While there was a respect (love) for both Cline's and Aeroquip's strengths, the overriding factor was my respect (love) for my own present position. I was given the low sales volume territory as a raw opportunity, not a plum.

As a general rule of thumb in progress, when things are at a standstill, nothing that exists from the past helps much. Selling, or persuading, is, in the purest sense of the word, getting things moving. Now, if you have something standing perfectly still there is only one of two reasons for it. Either no energy is being expended to move it, or there is something blocking the path, neutralizing the energy being applied. This can be, in its ultimate form, an irresistible force meeting an immovable object. Aeroquip and Cline were in this stalemate position.

Forward progress in stalled situations is usually only achieved by ignoring all previous attempts which failed, and trying something different. It's like a car that won't start. Fifteen people can try turning the key, but if the trouble is a dead battery, it doesn't make any sense for every new person arriving to just turn the key. Somebody has got to lift the hood.

Here is where the system for figuring things out is the tool to use. Doubt anything that feels comfortable to doubt, trust yourself, observe what is happening, and arrive at a truth. Truth is a motion, not a statue. Truth is only verifiable in action. State a truth, do nothing to prove it, and what have you got? A supposition. It is only truth when it is put into action and it works.

The laws of motion are the laws of truth, and both are equitable and fair. Movement is the desired goal of all energy, progress the desire for all initiative. When no progress is being made, as with Cline Company during ten stagnant years, the energy is being applied in the wrong direction.

All customers and prospects are in motion. They are either going my way, the other way, or circling around thinking about it. Nothing stands still. Now, if the customer is going away from me, there is still hope. You've seen the big stampede scene in the movies where the cowboy rides alongside the lead steers in the herd and influences them to change their direction. Sometimes the best way is to let the steer have his head for a few minutes. Just ride along, don't startle him further and gradually change the direction. At Cline Company, I sympathized with their irritation, or, in effect, ran alongside them in the same direction. This was easy enough to do, simply by seeing it from their perspective. Then, once accepted, I was in a position to help change the focus. The old focus was on the stalemate with my company. The new focus was on a harmony between all of us as people.

I didn't have a prayer of getting any motion going by putting some more energy into the concept of our two companies. The energy had to be applied between people. And when I gave them energy as people, note that I asked for a return of energy to me as a person.

This is what selling is all about. People.

CHAPTER 7

The System for Figuring Things Out

The first tool in the system for figuring things out is to doubt.

Doubt all you hear, see, think and feel if it feels comfortable to doubt it. Don't attack it. Just doubt it and relax and feel comfortable with your doubting process. Don't judge it or condemn it, for this is simply the extreme reverse of blindly following without doubt. Extremes are never comfortable. Above all, do not be angry with the supplier of the fact you are doubting, or with yourself for doubting.

Do not utilize the doubt in forming a position or too hastily reaching a decision.

Doubt is not a negative, but simply the step preceding either knowledge or acceptance. Many times a person will complete some difficult task or perform some physical feat and then say, "I didn't believe I could do it!" That "didn't believe" feeling is doubt. At other times a person may say, "I don't believe it will work," meaning, I do not see enough evidence of it being possible. If some evidence is found, the doubt disappears.

But in its first moment of arrival, doubt is simply the first stage leading toward further knowledge.

The second stage in figuring things out is trust.

Trust yourself. Don't tell anyone about it, but just quietly trust yourself. If you tell someone else you trust yourself they may ask you why and you may find yourself either defending yourself in some degree of desperation, because you haven't totally figured it out yet, or you may give up figuring it out and go back in the past to recall some great accomplishment to brag about. The reason you may do this is because all those other people have something they want you to trust and your trusting yourself often gets in their way.

Trust is a very private thing. Do it alone in silence even if you are talking with someone else at the time.

Even if you want some other opinions and ask people, never betray your trust in yourself. Ask them, "What do you do when this or that happens?" or, "How do you feel when such and such occurs?" Don't ask, "What do you think I ought to do?" If you ask that, you have given up your trust in yourself. Ask it the other way and trust yourself to consider their answer and maybe adapt it to your own situation. Maybe.

As you trust yourself, know you are two distinct persons. First, you are completely unique on this earth. No one else has ever walked, inch by inch, step by step, the exact precise path your life has followed to this point. Your experiences have shaped you as a person who is distinctive. Second, you are also a carbon copy of every other human being who ever walked this earth, all the way back to Noah and Moses and Adam. This strange dual role you play offers some real benefits. All feelings you have are similar to the feelings other people have, and their feelings are similar to ones you are capable of even if you don't feel them at this moment. Trust what you feel and trust yourself to acknowlege what the other person is feeling. And because you are unique, you may find a solution to the problem that the other person didn't conceive, though he can readily agree to it.

Trust everything you do not doubt. Do not make a decision to act yet, based on that trust, but trust. No matter what it is, if there is no doubt connected to it, trust it.

The third step in figuring things out is to observe.

The two elements to observe first are your doubt and trust. Play a mental, neutral game with them. The game is "What if?" What if your trust is misplaced, or your doubts unfounded? What if the thing you doubt is really true? What if you trust something that will not prove true? What if? The focal point of this game is to ask, what will happen if I doubt this and it proves true later? What position will I be in then? How will I be helped or hindered by how it comes out? If I go ahead and trust it or continue to doubt it?

Weigh all possibilities with a love of yourself and love for other people. Let go of your fear of the future while holding on to your awareness of hazards. Determine whether your options carry you directly into certain guaranteed harm from hazards or whether the hazards can be bypassed, however closely. What you are forming in this mental exercise is a calculated risk. There must be risk in all forward movement. Before this alarms you, know also the risks in retreating from opportunity. Calculate those risks carefully as well. Life is moving on in you and there is no place of absolute rest. You must either move forward or backwards. This does not, in itself, mean you must become more active, for it is possible to move forward to a peaceful calm as well as an energetic activity. But in whichever direction you move, do so without fear. Let go of fear and observe and utilize the four characteristics of love with yourself and the other person.

The real big ingredient of this doubt and trust and observation is that it is a continuous process. This is a plus in your life. You will not be bored by any day that arrives or any question it contains. You do not carry yesterday's truth forward to today as though it were an absolute. Actually, there is a pretty fair chance for happiness today also, because yesterday's error produced only a learning experience, or truth, and none of it has to be allowed to regulate today. You are totally free to decide today's questions by today's truth.

The fourth step in figuring things out is truth. Not doubt, trust or observation. Truth.

The system doesn't have any short-cuts. And the system doesn't provide any truth before you use steps one, two and three. In fact, if you try to short-cut the game, and seize a truth as step one, all you get is some stale, left-over truth from some past experience. This old truth never fits in perfectly with the issue at hand. In the principle of motion, we all grow every day and trust and doubt new things all the time as they arrive. So the old truth needs to be updated and changed slightly or tremendously to fit what is happening right now. Sometimes the best way is to look for a brand new truth, then say, "Ah! Yes! This is a bit similar to that older truth." When you do it this way you don't have to fight the authority of all past truths.

So when you have something to figure out, avoid truths like the plague until you have doubted, trusted, and observed. After you have done all that, truth will arrive. If it arrives too soon it may be an old truth and you may wish to treat it like a wrong bus approaching. Step back from the curb and wave the driver on by. Don't worry. Your correct bus will arrive in a moment.

This sounds like a wavering, purposeless confusion. It really isn't, for you trust yourself, and this one fact alone prevents confusion in any anxious way. You may have a period of ignorance in the form of not knowing what to do, but ignorance is not confusion. Confusion only arises from feeling or deciding a move must be made immediately, before it is known exactly what that move could or should be. Is this not so? So relax with your system of figuring it out and go ahead and doubt, trust and observe.

CHAPTER 8

The Hidden Tool

Re-examining the situation at Cline Company, there is one aspect of this sales conversation with Neb Cline, Jr. that was peculiar. Did you spot it? Neb handed me a relatively nice stock order and I began looking at the windows. How about that for an irrelevant reaction? Doesn't make any sense, does it?

Can you imagine a sales manager training a staff of salesmen and instructing them, "Now, when your prospect gives you the order, look at the window"? So why did I do such a crazy thing?

It came about after I stood there empty, with absolutely no knowledge of how to get started on the next words with Neb. Not knowing what to say, I was concentrating on Neb and the situation and what I hoped he would do, which was to get committed to some serious work with me.

Neb had been pleasant as we had had lunch a time or two, and we had talked about a lot of different things besides just business. Sharing a few jokes, we kidded about a lot of miscellaneous, irrelevant subjects. So, I knew Neb a little bit, and when I stood there looking at that order some inner voice said, "Jar him. In a nice, friendly way, provoke him into some deeper thought. He is too pat, too complacent with his handing you the order. He has finally accepted you, and that's nice, but is he ready to move on the sales plan? The rhythm of his words implied that my reaction should be to say, 'Thank you.' But 'Thank you' doesn't get our bigger plans moving."

My third eye put that action into use and selected those words. Does this sound crazy to you? I've made a lot of sales by using statements or questions that don't seem to make real sense to me later. Yet at the exact moment of the empty feeling I had as I searched for a remark or an action, the third eye was taking control of the situation.

I believe the third eye takes into consideration not only my emotions but also the emotions of the person I am talking to and the details or realities of the situation we are both experiencing, and then computes and hands me a remark to fit in with the mood of what is happening. I also believe that for it to happen I've got to be paying real close attention to that other person and operate from a base of love for people. I've got to know the other person, accept them as they are at the exact moment, be concerned for the way our transaction is proceeding, and be committed to doing whatever is required to move the situation forward, no matter how crazy or unorthodox that action might be. I've got to be operating emotionally in the exact present time, not thinking of some great remark from the past.

If I am operating from some opinionated stance and have already formed a remark or two before the transaction begins, then the third eye goes on strike and will not work. The third eye seems to either want to be in charge or be absent, one of the two. It always works out that the third eye will not compute unless I go totally empty and give it control. Then, and only then, will it hand me the correct words to speak.

The third eye is the final step in the system for figuring things out. All the doubt, trust and observation has been happening, and either I haven't found the truth yet, or if I've found the truth, I'm having a hard time speaking about it. So instead of forming a comment that doesn't really have much relevance to the exact situation, I stand there empty. Then some words come to me that often surprise me as much as the other person who hears them.

When you have a situation that is becoming difficult and you do not know what to say next and you want to be fair and also handle the situation with effectiveness and fairness to yourself also, then turn loose of all thought. Go completely empty in your mind. And when you are empty, an inner voice will speak to you and tell you the words to say. That voice will be the voice of love. Listen to what it is telling you to do or say. Now, right behind that first inner voice, you will hear another voice telling you that what you heard from the first voice will not work. This second voice is the voice of fear. Listen to the voice of love, do as it instructs, and you will be able to do your job well.

If you conceive the inner voice to be some word such as cosmic energy, intuition, sixth sense, or a thousand other names, that is the force that selects the words. There is a positive force and you are as good at naming it as I am. Just know that when you go empty you will receive some words to use. The alternative to being filled with some words to use is to remain empty, and since you are not a can of coffee or peanuts, you are not vacuum-packed. Something will come to you when you are not sealed up.

CHAPTER 9

A Novel Chart

As a salesman, your greatest enemies are your ego, your pride, the personal internal impression you have of needing to prove yourself, and that sales chart on the wall, the one that judges everyone by pitting them against each other instead of just against their own personal limitations.

Once, the Monroe Company brought out a huge merchandise package to be sold to dealers at a cost of over $1,200. Imagine it! We had been selling a package for three or four years that cost less than $300.

At the sales meeting a curtain was closed up on stage, same as usual. Fanfare was being generated to build up excitement in the men as we waited for a look at this year's deal. The music began. Monroe, being a first class company, had some live musicians for the fanfare.

Suddenly, I turned and elbowed Jack Mitchell, my district manager. "Jack, this deal is going to be unbelievable in size!"

"Why do you say that?"

"Count the musicians. This year we've grown from three to seven."

Jack laughed. Then the curtain opened and we saw the big deal.

Everyone drew in their breath, and the same question reverberated around in everyone's mind. How can we sell a $1,200 package to the man who needed a lot of conversation to purchase the deal one-fifth that size?

When the meeting ended, back in the territory, I began by calling on the best single dealer I had in the state. He sold shocks daily. I didn't know how I would tell him about the package. Oh, I had a beautiful picture of the stock cabinet, a list of the merchandise in it, a price sheet, some extended terms to make the price easier, and some special tools to make installation easier, but that was nothing more than the details. What I didn't know was what element my dealer would find in himself to make him want it.

"Hi, Clyde."

"Hi, Chuck. How's it been?"

"Good. How 'bout you? What have you been up to lately?"

"I've been fine. Been doing a little fishing. Say, are you here to sell me one more barrel deal?"

"Well, no. But don't knock it. You've sold a lot of shocks using those barrels."

"Yeah. But, you know, Chuck, those deals are not so hot for us, in a way."

"Why?"

"Well, it is a shot in the arm for a dealer to get started by selling a dozen shocks. But we have a big shop here and a dozen shock absorbers might not last two days. So you come around every year and we buy a barrel deal, with Ford, Chevy and Plymouth shocks in it. The next customer to come in is driving a Buick, and the shocks in the barrel won't fit it. We are no better off than when we started."

"Well, Clyde, what do you think would be the ideal answer to the problem?"

"I don't know, exactly. We just pick them up from the jobber after we get the car on the rack and find the shocks need replacing. I'm not going to buy another barrel, because the car on the rack isn't always a Ford, Chevy or Plymouth."

"How much time does it take you to go get the shocks from the jobber?"

"Depends on who we send and how long it's been since their last coffee break, and how busy the jobber counter-men are when he gets there. Anywhere from twenty minutes to forty-five."

"Do you get to charge the customer extra for this expense?"

"Are you kidding? That's overhead. Strictly un-chargeable."

"You know, Clyde, maybe the company could figure out some way to put a big stock of shocks in your place here and extend some longer terms for payment. If they did you could have all the shocks you need without shell-ing out a lot of money up front."

"Now, that wouldn't be too bad. But how would Monroe ever extend terms to a dealer? You sell to the wholesaler and the wholesaler sells to me."

"It would take a special setup, all right. But if that setup were available to you, would you be interested?"

"You bet!"

"Clyde, let me show you something brand new from Monroe."

He purchased the $1,200 deal. Purchased? He sold me on it too! Using pretty much the same kind of backing into the conversation style, I sold fourteen of those deals that month, going to just the better dealers, picking my places carefully.

At a district sales meeting at the end of the month, Jack went around the room and asked each salesman in the district, "How many of the big deals did you sell this month?" Everyone said, "None." Then with a devilish gleam in his eye Jack said, "Chuck, tell us what kind of hard work and perseverance it took for you to sell four-teen of them." My buddies drew in their breath and muttered. After the buzz died down I said, "When there ever gets to be the slightest sign of hard work involved in this job, I plan to resign at once." Now the room didn't buzz. It laughed. Me too. That former buzz had some very natural resentment in it. These were my friends.

Suddenly, without really intending to make it into a negative, Jack had positioned it where it was making them look like maybe they hadn't given any "hard work and perseverance." Jack picked it up again, after the laugh. "O.K. Then would you please tell us what stroke of sheer laziness produced those sales?" Some more laugh-ter, and all the resentment was gone. After I recounted the conversation with my customers everybody laughed again. The other salesmen went out and outsold me the following month, using the same approach. Clyde gave them their clue.

The point to this little incident is that all of us had been jacked up full of good intentions about hard work before we went out to sell that big deal. The other men had more self-confidence than I did, and they went out like John Wayne to do the job. Being ignorant, I stumbled into Clyde's place and fumbled around until he told me how he wanted to buy it. I knew I couldn't sell anything to anybody, and I was concerned also that Clyde wouldn't buy it. The other salesmen, as they admitted they had sold none, also stated how hard they worked trying to sell the deals. One man said, "I talked until I was blue in the face."

When we counted score at that sales meeting, it was like when a sales manager puts a big chart on the wall with everyone's name on it, then writes in the sales beside each man's name. The salesmen on the bottom of the chart feel bad, and the ones on the top often have a slight problem with their egos.

I've thought about this a lot. My name has been on a lot of charts and as a sales manager I've also used the charts. And the internal results in the salesmen are nearly the same in most instances. The big sellers miss some sales when their name hits the top line of the chart because they read the chart and say, "Hey! I must have it figured out! I'll just do it that exact same way again next month!" Then next month they sound like a record player and wonder how those buyers slipped through their fingers.

Life seems to have a cycle effect. First a man knows nothing, then struggles to learn, allowing the world to teach him. Achieving success, he feels great, decides he can do without his teachers, and begins missing some good lessons. He then has a decline and finds, once again, he knows nothing, and allows his teachers to educate him all over again. It all keeps turning in his head. And the reason it perpetuates in this endless circle is because of two elements. Pride and ego. A beginner will usually swallow his pride and listen. Later, he won't if he lets his ego control him. A phrase often heard from someone in this self-elevated position is, "Do you know who you are talking to?"

Now, I'm not saying that the whole natural system of the human ego can be repealed. How are we going to do that? No, we are what we are, and the ego is part of us. So is pride. At a glance, it doesn't appear that any solution to this up and down cycle is available, does it?

How about this for a try? Why can't we learn to be proud of our ignorance? How do you feel about that? Undecided?

Well, how about our defining ignorance a little more so

we can think about it some more. O.K.? I don't think ignorance means stupidity, and I don't think humility means a denial of any good points in ourselves. I'd like to believe I'm not stupid and I'd like to believe I've got some good points.

So, how about considering ignorance as just the step in the cycle before knowledge? Like, do you know how to juggle three objects in the air? No? Well, I didn't either. I was ignorant. Not stupid. Just ignorant. But I saw a friend doing that and just for the pure curiosity of it I bought three little juggle bags filled with beans or peas or sand or whatever is in there I don't know. I read the instruction sheet, and that was really as much help as a diagram for assembling something printed in Chinese. Anyway, I had a go at juggling. Lost four pounds and toned up, just bending over to pick up the dropped bags. Still ignorant. Then I stood over the couch to try it, so the dropped bags could be retrieved with a half-bend. Then a friend juggled again for me and gave me a few tips and I began juggling just fine now that I had some more knowledge. One minor problem. I spent a month learning how to do it. Now that I know how, doing it for more than three seconds in a row seems kind of silly.

The point is, ignorance is a temporary condition while stupidity sometimes can be a lifelong habit. A little knowledge will cure ignorance, but stupidity is an emotional disease. Ignorance exists in the mind, stupidity in the soul. Stupidity can be cured only in solitude, rethinking. But ignorance can be cured with other people, watching, listening and using the system for figuring things out.

Now, my ego is still intact, and I've got to find an outlet for it. I've got to be good at something, otherwise, on a comparative scale, I'm a "loser." Incidentally, while we often group ourselves using name tags of "winners" and "losers," and allow our egos to shrink or expand, a winner is a person whose loss very possibly lies around the corner and a loser is someone possibly proceeding in the opposite direction. Knowing this makes it a little foolish for either to thumb his nose at the other in passing, doesn't it?

Looking around at all this, the comparative rating chart business seems to be risky. If I participate in it and wallow in my self-concept as I read it on the chart, whether I'm at the top or the bottom puts me in some risk. I may either give up learning because I wonder if I'll ever make it or give up learning because I think I've got it made. Either way, my refusal to continue to learn is stupid, isn't it? I've already decided I don't want to be stupid, so I'll ignore the comparative chart as I take stock of myself and form my self-picture as accurately as I can.

But giving up the chart isn't a positive action, just a letting go, and my ego demands an accomplishment, something positive to brag about. The ego always has to brag. When it does, I lose, because I lose my ignorance or at least my ego tells me I have lost it and so I stop using it. Maybe the words of the puzzle also contain the solution, if I just put all the pieces together correctly. That's the way it usually is. Remove 17 pieces out of a box that says, "1,297 piece jigsaw puzzle," and what have you got? Garbage. It's only a puzzle when all the pieces are there. So here I am with my puzzle. I've got an ego. I've got ignorance. Ah! I've got it! I'll become proud of my ignorance! Why didn't I think of this before? Possibly because I was ignorant, and I didn't investigate it thoroughly. But now that I've asked myself all these questions I've discovered the knowledge, which is that my ignorance is the best shot I can take with my ego.

But wait. How will this fit me in with my peer group and

my customers? They are always like I am, wanting to be best at something or another. We all have these egos. This is going to fit in perfectly! They will be knowledgeable, I'll be ignorant, and it will all fit together. We'll get along just fine. I'll ask a quesion, and they will answer it. I've demonstrated my ignorance and they have demonstrated their knowledge. Also, this system has a hidden, built-in benefit. When two people meet and talk, the listener learns something while the talker is stuck with a rerun of a previous knowledge.

Now, how do I keep this thing under control? How can I avoid getting my name so high on the list of ignorant people that my ignorance becomes too great and defeats me? That's easy. There is no list of ignorant people. The FBI has a list of the ten most wanted people, but no agency keeps a list of the ten most ignorant people. Just about every company keeps a list of the top producers, but no list of the top ignorant people. So, I don't actually have to prove my ignorance to anyone. In fact, most people don't want to hear about it. Can you imagine idly dropping this following tidbit into social conversation at a party? "I'm going to Acapulco next month as a prize I won for being the most ignorant man in my company."

Incidentally, I have no risk at all in offering you this device to salve your ego. You are not going to brag about your ignorance either. You will never threaten me with some idle one-upmanship ego game of pursuit of maximum ignorance on the comparative scale. But now I'm at the top of the ignorance chart and still do not lose the thing that made me great to begin with at the start. And since I'm the only person on my self-designed ignorance chart I don't have to pose and posture and strut with it. I can spend all that energy just using the great reservoir of ignorance. Want to see how it looks in action again?

100

The Marriott Hotel in downtown Atlanta refurbished its kitchen and many of its rooms. I overheard that they had a warehouse full of furnishings they wished to sell. Now, right there was my first genius stroke of master ignorance. Ignorant people listen. It's just when I'm both stupid and ignorant that I fail to hear.

Wearing sandals, jeans, flowing shirt, bead necklace, long hair and beard which I had grown for the bicentennial year, I entered their offices. A secretary asked, "May I help you?" in the same tone of voice she might have said, "Are you lost?" I was in the pottery business then, and the nearly hippie get-up was just fine for that atmosphere, even if a little casual for the Marriott offices.

"I heard you have some furnishings to sell. Is that correct?"

"Yes. I'll let you talk to Pete Henry."

When Pete appeared we shook hands and I repeated the question. He affirmed it.

"Would you please take me to them?"

He took me across the street, unlocked a door, and ushered me into a big storage room situated at street level underneath a multi-storied parking lot. This place was loaded with everything. I didn't know the first thing about any of it. I looked for a moment and then asked Pete, "Would you lock that door behind you and come back in an hour? I need to look at this very carefully." He snapped the padlock back in place and returned to his office. I was alone with the weirdest assortment of goods imaginable. There were about 500 banquet chairs, a life guard's chair, some huge chandeliers about thirteen or fourteen feet in diameter, kitchen equipment, guest room furniture, and on and on it went, as high as it could be stacked in that room.

I asked myself, what would I do with this, me being the

Marriott Hotel managers and employees? I'm a hotel management expert now, in my mind, so what do I do with some worn goods? How do I get rid of them, and when I do, how do I get a fair price?

The single fact I possessed was a very small knowledge of a few salvage operators in Atlanta who purchased large lots of goods like this pile in front of me. But I'm not a salvage operator. For fifteen or twenty minutes I just looked at everything, slowly walking around. Then I got busy and began making a detailed list of the room's contents. Pete came back just as I was finishing.

"Pete, before we discuss this, you might want to take a look at these two items. Here is a full set of maintenance tools and a brand new employees time clock still in the original shipping case. Looks to me like you would be better off keeping these useful items. What do you think?"

"I think you are right! I wonder how these got in this pile of goods?"

"How about having a cup of coffee with me and I'll make you a proposition?"

"O.K."

Settled in over coffee, I said, "Pete, there are three ways for you to sell those goods. First, you can sell it all in one shot to a salvage operator. Just taking a guess from this inventory sheet I'd say a salvager will offer you two or three thousand dollars for all of it. The second way to sell is to put one of your employees on it and let him sell it a piece at a time. If you do it that way you can get ten times the amount you would from salvage. The only drawback is that you need a good man to do it and you can kiss him goodbye from his regular hotel job until he is through with the project. The third way is to let me sell it for you. I don't have storage space for it, so I'll have to sell it right from that storage room of yours. First we can double check this inventory and make sure it's accurate. Then when I sell items we can check them off the list. This will work if you don't need to have that room totally emptied for a month or so. When I sell the items at the higher price, I'll keep thirty-three cents on the dollar as my commission, and you get sixty-seven cents on the dollar. This whole thing can be a handshake deal if you like it and if you don't like the way it is proceeding you are free to stop at any moment. Just as a guess, you should get ten times as much money out of the goods this way without disrupting your employees' other responsibilities. How do you feel about it?"

"Will you wait here and finish your coffee while I check something?"

"Sure."

Five minutes later he returned with a smile on his face.

"We've got a deal. I conferred with another man in the office. The thing that swung the deal is that I believe you are honest. Otherwise, you would have kicked those tools and that clock up under a stack of goods and maybe just let it be our loss in some way."

After a month of selling, without neglecting my normal, regular business, Pete had twenty thousand dollars in proceeds and I had ten, some of which I shared with an auctioneer. I sold the items down to a hard core of difficult pieces, then let the professional auctioneer move them under his gavel.

The whole point about ignorance, and what makes it such a beautiful tool, is that I never questioned my inexperience in the salvage business. The trouble with all these social and professional codes of experience, intelligence, and everything having a set of absolute ways it has got to proceed, is that there is no room in there anywhere for ignorance or curiosity or trying new things. Like, when I used an auctioneer, a written contract was required, by law. The auctioneer's lawyer, very experienced and knowledgeable, said no one would ever sign an auction contract at a thirty-three percent commission rate because the standard auction commission was much lower. I guess that's right. I don't know. I'm not in the auction business. But the deal I had with Pete had me in for a third of the sales price, whether I needed a written piece of paper for the auctioneer or not. So I asked the lawyer to be the lawyer and let me be the person doing the business. I'd trust him to get all the commas and whereas clauses right and he would have to trust me to get the thing signed. And in that auction contract, I had a fifty percent share of the auction commission.

The whole deal was a lot of fun. I've never done it again. It was just something to do with a chance overheard bit of information. Being ignorant, I didn't realize I couldn't do it and when I started I had no idea how to gain Pete Henry's attention and had to stand in that storage room one whole hour asking myself questions and guessing at answers. Then I had to scratch my head again and get the assistance of the auctioneer who had more knowledge than I did about selling the more difficult items.

The stroke of pure luck, of course, was finding that time clock and set of tools. I didn't know I would do that, but it was the key to the whole deal being accepted. But I didn't even know it was the key. I just found the items and because the customer was about to have a loss, I called his attention to it, not knowing it was the key to the agreement. That is maximum ignorance.

What ignorance really means, in the truest sense, is a neutrality. I do not know, therefore I cannot judge. I don't know if the customer will or will not buy from me, so I do not judge him in advance when I knock on his door. Also, I don't know if I can solve his problem until I see the problem. This ignorance prevents me from judging my ability or myself in any way. I am curious to see what happens. Further, I do not know what aspect of the situation will allow me to offer a value that causes an acceptance, because I do not know any of the details.

Neutrality does not mean loss of purpose. In the components of love, there is knowledge, acceptance, concern and commitment. To achieve this transaction with Pete Henry I had to commit to getting into the rare confusion he was experiencing, by placing myself in his shoes, accepting his position, pretending I was a hotel executive with the used goods on my hands, concerned about the problems he faced. In this way, we must identify so closely with the prospect that we become one with them and their problems. Once this happens, the committed salesman can struggle through the confusion and lead the prospect out of it also. The key word is lead, not push.

Let's look at ignorance again, this time in a situation where I was supposedly, on the surface of it, an "expert."

One customer, Tamper, Inc., was just getting started with a new manufacturing plant. They were builders of the world's finest machines to maintain railway tracks and roadbeds. You may have seen these large machines out on railroad tracks. They are as big as a bulldozer and are highly complicated, having a maze of hydraulic lines so profuse that the inner workings of the machine resembles a bowl of spaghetti.

When I approached Tamper, Inc. I was apprehensive at first, for their engineering staff surely must be brilliant, and here I was fresh out of a ninety day school for just the hydraulic lines. I decided to trust Aeroquip to have trained me well and therefore trust my ability. When I met the purchasing agent, Bill Minnick, I asked if I could be taken to their assembly line to examine their machines. Bill consented. Once on the line I discovered that in one area, no exact fitting had been available to connect two components, and so to solve a problem, six fittings had been screwed together in order to achieve the correct configuration. I quickly made a drawing of just one fitting which would replace the six, went to a phone, called Aeroquip's engineering department and obtained a quotation on the special fitting. Presenting this to Bill Minnick, we discovered that the one fitting saved 60 percent in costs by eliminating five unnecessary parts, while also eliminating five steps in assembly and also improving the reliability of the machine.

Bill ordered the new special fittings, and also gave me a $12,000 order for the first month's supply of all other items I sold which would be needed on the assembly line.

The point is, I was totally ignorant when it began. I had no knowledge of the problem Tamper was facing, and discovered it by a simple encounter of a machine being built on the assembly line. The factory school had filled me with knowledge, but this knowledge was simply a set of dry facts having no importance until a customer's problem was encountered. To discover the problem, I had to begin in ignorance.

Now watch what happens when I get all full of myself and forget that my natural condition is ignorance.

Tamper had another technical problem some months later and requested some consideration be given to modifying our product slightly to better fit their exact needs. To expedite matters, I asked the concerned persons to come into Bill Minnick's office where we could all speak to an engineer at the Aeroquip plant. Bill had a loudspeaker phone on his desk, and as I placed the call I began feeling my importance.

"This will be easy. We work very closely with our engineers and they will be happy to hear the problem and eager to solve it."

About this time the Aeroquip engineer I had asked for was connected. I gave the Tamper men a confident, reassuring look as the voice on the other end spoke to all of us through the loudspeaker.

"Hello."

"Hello, Joe. This is Chuck Lewis."

"Chuck who?"

Men began doubling up with it. Me too. When I found my voice I said, "Joe, you just blew my image."

It was a gas, but it didn't end there. Bill Minnick is devilishly clever and he found a way to rib me about that call for months afterward, even before I got to his office.

I'd present myself to his receptionist, who phoned him to say, "Chuck Lewis to see you."

Pause.

"Lewis."

Finally she stated, after twenty more visits, "Bill has a hard time getting your last name."

"Yeah. I know. Fellow up at my plant has the same problem."

CHAPTER 10

Plow Mules
and Snowflakes

There is a system for power selling. There is also a system
for ignorance. If you want to power sell, play the numbers game. Get up every day, pick your attitude and stick
with it. If you choose to be cheerful, grin at every last
human being you see that day. During the course of the
day, if you move fast, you will meet a lot of people. A few
of them will relate perfectly to whichever mood you have
chosen. You will get along just fine with these few and
they will buy your idea or product. That is selling. And it
is the hardest work you will ever find. You have to see
twenty times as many people as the non-salesman. And all
those people who reject you hurt you inside in your ego.
You will begin doubting yourself and resenting them.
When this happens you will probably look around for a
"winner" approach—some deft pattern of words that
seem likely to succeed. When you use them, many people
will still reject you and your idea. The next step is to think
a lot about noble, hard work. You will become like a good
plow mule, blindly walking straight ahead pulling the
burden of your sharp, pointed plow. When it digs into an
obstruction you will grunt even harder and strain to move
the obstruction. Whether you are successful or not you
will be in a sweat. A lot of good men have gone out there
and pulled that same plow and quit in disgust or fatigue.

The other way, not selling, but looking around for buyers, asking questions to discover their desires, wording your appeals to fit their moods, frowning with them over problems, smiling with them over solutions, being ignorant when it begins and not having your ego out there on the line, you will find buyers in very surprising places. Many people will purchase from you while you are still scratching your head trying to figure out how and why it happened.

When your sales manager or the company president slaps you on the back, resist your ego. The surest way you can fail now is to say, "Wow! I must be terrific!" If you say that, even privately, you may lose your ignorance and approach the next prospect too full of yourself and your past accomplishments. Life isn't some great snowball you roll down a hill gathering size. It is the individual snowflakes, each one different, one falling here, one there, one in your eyebrow, another on your nose. Try to feel each one of them as a separate experience. It is all new. The only wisdom is that there is no wisdom. The only truth is the truth of this exact moment. Tomorrow, you will have lived with today's truth for twenty-four hours and it will be just slightly different because your experience of it will grow as you reflect on it and see it from various perspectives.

When you look back at your successes, try not to remember the results as much as the process. Remember your confusion as you stood perplexed trying to figure it all out. If you have any asset to carry forward it is simply the sure knowledge that you have to figure it out again and again and again and you have the tools of doubt, trust, and observation to lead you to truth, whatever the question is in front of you. Forget yesterday's solution. This is today and today demands a fresh start. If there is a great similarity between today's problem and yesterday's solution, relax and let it happen, but don't force it to happen in the exact same way it occurred yesterday. Above all, don't plan to use it automatically again tomorrow. Let tomorrow take care of itself, and it will when it arrives if you carry doubt, trust and observation into it.

Love yourself and the people you meet, with knowledge gained by inquiry and observation, concern for the welfare of both of you, a commitment to new truths as you find them, and a commitment to your prospect's problems. Take great care to forgive the errors each of you may make. Give an open acceptance to the day, yourself and the other person.

Cherish your ignorance and listen to the voice in you that speaks of love. Do what it tells you. The surest indication of your being on the right track is when it feels new to you.

CHAPTER 11

Let's Sell Something

All this stating of principles is just fine, but it doesn't pay the rent. So let's get in the middle of the action and use some of the principles with some real prospects.

As we approach these prospects, the system for planned ignorance is now working in us. The first step in the system of planned ignorance is to remove all conceptions from the mind and allow the prospect to implant and insert fresh data in the first instant of meeting. To do this correctly, or ignorantly, look at everything in your surroundings and the prospect's surroundings as though you were a farm boy who just stepped off the bus in downtown New York. You look at everything. While you look, you trust yourself. Buried in your subconscious mind is a gut feeling about many facets of human nature. You have carefully considered the realities of the system for figuring things out and the human interplay as people adapt the system for figuring things out to their individual peculiarities and personalities. Your third eye is a friend, and will assist you if you accept this helper. You are willing to go empty and wait for the inner voice to speak to you. You trust this inner voice.

O.K.? Ready? Here come the prospects. This is a real situation. It happened in Atlanta at the Atlanta Motor Home Show. Oh, by the way, you are going to make the sale. My part in this is just to talk a little with your subconscious mind, your emotions, and your third eye. Relax. I made the sale once, now we will both make it together. That's it. Now you are in the right frame of mind. You don't know how you are going to make a sale, and you don't know who the customer is yet, but you got up this morning and said, "There is a lot of advertising for this show. People should come out in good numbers. I'm going to do my best to find a few buyers in that crowd."

Here comes a couple. Middle-aged, tanned, wearing jackets with all manner of camper patches on them, smiling at everything. Our prospects? Maybe. But that smile looks too easygoing, and how about all those patches? I bet they will talk to you, but will it be an opportunity to sell, or just a pleasant time-killing conversation? You want to try? O.K. But find out about all those patches and that too perfect relaxation and do it in a quick way.

Give them a smile and ask, "What kind of motor home do you folks have?"

Wait. You say, why not start with "hello"? Well, you did that with your smile. And how about "hello"? Some two-hour conversations begin with "hello." Have you got two hours to spare? This opener gets them into stating their business, fast. And look, they are responding to you and your smile.

"We've got a Discoverer." Can you hear that pride and satisfaction in it? And gee, look at those grins. These people are here to look around. Nothing more. If they were unhappy or considering a trade they wouldn't be grinning quite that hard. You want to check them out a little further? O.K.

"Had it long?"

"A year. We go everywhere in it. Last month we went to Disneyland. Had a dickens of a time."

"Great!" Hey, you did that just right. You said "great" just before they could tell you the name of the campground they used, the route they drove, the gas they consumed, and the cuteness of their granddaughter who they saw for the first time in Jacksonville. Now right behind that "great!" establish some business before they get to all those details.

"Is there anything about your Discoverer you would change if you could?"

"No, it's terrific."

"Great! Enjoy the show! Thanks for coming!" Now take one step in any direction except toward them, and break eye contact. Leave your smile on. It isn't rude. It's been a pleasant exchange, you've found them to be easy-going talkers, and extracted yourself from an involvement that has no profit in it. You say you don't understand that question about changing their Discoverer if they could? No, we don't want to repair their Discoverer or remodel it, but we do take them in on trade. O.K.? You say it isn't fair? If they want to talk we should talk? Well, maybe. But look, right in the next booth, they have a real conversation going already. That salesman isn't going to sell them either, but he will spend twenty minutes finding that out.

Meanwhile, the people keep on moving through those front doors. The attendance at this show may reach as high as 30,000 people, maybe more. There are eleven exhibitors. Last year, the best selling exhibitor sold 27 units at the show. This year if every exhibitor sells 27, that comes to 297 units. A little arithmetic tells you that one out of every hundred people who attend will buy a unit, maybe less of a ratio if it rains this weekend and everybody looks for some indoor fun. When it rains they come to these indoor shows in droves.

So what's the clue to use in finding the buyer? Well, take that couple over there with the three kids. They are whizzing around looking at everything in sight, but did you hear their comments? "Gee, these things are really luxurious, aren't they?" "Yeah! Terrific!" "Hey, Mom, look! Look at the kitchen in this one!" You think they would buy? They are tire kickers, here just to see what it is all about. They may settle down and get interested, but right now they are fresh full of gee whiz and golly without a slightest personal interest in actually owning a unit. You can sell them, but you have to start at square one. Then when you finish, they have to think about it and won't sign the order.

In contrast, see that couple over there, opening that storage door on that coach? They are past the glitter and dazzle stage of the first moment of gee whiz and golly and ain't it all grand. They are looking at that storage hole as though they know exactly what they want to put in it. Maybe a pair of lawn chairs and a barbecue grill. Let's go and see—oops! Too late. There's Frank saying hello to them already, and look, Jim and Paul were also having a polite foot race to get over there quick. Well, when we snooze we lose.

In between the intent interest of that couple Frank is talking to and the glazed-eyed wonder of that nice family of friendly gawkers, there are other clues to look for in the crowd. Watch the eyes, hands and the posture. The ones coming through too relaxed, looking like they are on a pleasant stroll, eyes just taking it all in, pausing now and then to point from a distance at some novel feature, never touching any of the equipment; those are tourists in the show. It is a way to kill the afternoon. They may troop in and out of twenty motor homes, but they are here to look, not buy.

But watch for the ones whose pace varies, whose conferences with their mate in the aisles and displays find them leaning toward each other in more intensity or interest, whose gestures are specific and not always toward some funny feature, but maybe pointing to a bed arrangement or table feature, whose steps take them closer to the details, hands reaching to touch, heads bending down to see how concealed hinges work, hands exploring things in greater detail, gaze reflective, the look on the face maybe a little serious, as though they are really thinking about something. Those are the buyers. If they find the exact thing that fits their mood they will buy.

What's that? You say only about one of twenty people look like that? Congratulations! You are getting the message.

Another thing, you are standing in the middle of your display or at the aisle, and someone comes into view too fast for you to have watched them at all. Suddenly there they are in front of you. You have one split second to appraise them. Take it all in, and zero in on their eyes and mouth. There is a set to the eyes and mouth that says buyer, shopper, or time killer.

You say, "Hey, wait! Awhile back, in the book, in the

figuring things out part, it said look at everything. Now here are these narrowed-down clues. Isn't this just some grand advance truth without all the steps to figure it out, you know: doubt, trust, and observation? And how about general curiosity? You are putting signs and labels on these people pretty quickly, aren't you?"

Well, yes, and no. They put their own signs on themselves. Like, when you make a sales call on a big industrial plant, and the receptionist sends you into a room to see your prospect. On the door, the name plate says, "Joe Smith, Purchasing Agent." You go in and the sign on the desk says, "Joe Smith, Purchasing Agent." And there sits Joe, and guess what? All you have done is get to the right place to start. All the doubt, trust and observation are still ahead of you in the conversation. It's the same at this show. The people give you the signs: buyer, shopper, or tire kicker. But the work is still all there in front of you. All we have done at this stage of the game is make sure we didn't get lost and wind up in the wrong place.

Talking to a tire kicker is like trying to sell a new computer to the sanitation supervisor in a big company. So we pick out a person who looks like a buyer. All the work is still in front of us to do. All we have exercised so far is our third eye.

And see that salesman at the next booth? He just finished talking to the couple with the big grins and all those camper patches. He spent twenty-five minutes finding out he couldn't sell them a replacement for that Discoverer they love so well. In the process, he heard more about their trip to Disneyland than he really wanted to know. Look at the expression on his face. You think maybe his third eye is beginning to get activated? He is flinching about his lost time and energy.

In reality, we have doubted and trusted and observed, though, even though it all happened at a distance. You might say, well, we spent all this time looking at the crowd and at least that other salesman is no worse off, because we both have talked to just one pair of prospects, the Discoverer owners.

Well, there is another point right there. This crowd is exciting in a way, confusing in a way, and overpowering in a way. So what we have done is settle into the crowd mentally and emotionally, get our bearings, and figure things out as to our first step. Now we know, pretty much, which people to approach. Don't worry about our lost time. We will save it back fifteen times before the weekend is over just by knowing what we are looking for and not spending time with the wrong people.

The other thing is our mood. While that salesman who is wrestling with his third eye feels a little confusion right now, we feel a sense of purpose. Look, there he goes again. Look at that gee whiz, golly, ain't it all wonderful pair of tire kickers he is approaching. Oh! Great! Did you see that? They quickly said, "We're just looking," and breezed right by him. Did him a favor. Now watch him. He'll pick his next prospect and his next words a little more carefully. That third eye is talking to him. If he listens to it he'll make it. If he doesn't, he'll starve to death on that job.

The main trouble or problem with talking to every single person without any distinction is that it is too easy to never really say anything that matters to anybody. In this way a salesman at a show can become like a social butterfly at a large party. Sure, everyone gets a smile, but no one really gets to share anything of thought-inducing relevance. Please don't misunderstand. I do that at a party sometimes, too. You know, grin and say "hi" to

119

everyone. When I do, it is usually because I don't know what to say to any one person that would mean anything to them. I found a cure for that, though, by learning to listen to what someone else wanted to say. Now, not only did this give me some information, but it also triggers a response from me and this response becomes something of meaning to the other person. The encounter begins to achieve some substance this way.

It's the same at this show. How can we know what to say to everyone of these people? And why should we try? Why not let them talk to us with their gestures and moods and posture and actions? Then we can speak to them with some relevance to their thinking process. If we do this, we won't be social butterflies at the show, we will be purchasing helpers, or, if your ego simply must use the word, salesmen. How do you feel about that?

The first step in this selling game is prospects. When I make industrial sales calls I drive into a town and pick out the biggest company who uses, or could use, a product I sell. When I'm in Atlanta, that's General Motors or Coca-Cola or Lockheed Aircraft or Southern Railway, or Mead Packaging. I once spent three solid days in the main offices of Coca-Cola selling an improved paper for their copy machines. Every time I went into another office to see another department head, I was asked, "Have a Coke?" I said, "Sure!" What was I supposed to say, something like, "No, give me a Pepsi," or, "Do you have any milk?" I fizzed inside for twenty-four hours. The second day I snooped around and got the biggest bottle of Coke I could find and carried it around with me all day long in and out of all those offices. The first day, these people had pushed a button under their desk top and a woman had come in with a Coke for me. I drank twelve of them, smacked my lips over every one, and percolated like a time bomb. The second day, when I entered, I said, "Don't push the buzzer. I brought my own." They found out I was working all the offices and laughed about it. My fizz subsided to a normal level.

But the point is to always get to the biggest or best or most promising prospect you can find. It's the same at this motor home show. Once we find a prospect who shows any sign of being willing to convert from prospect to customer we can spend as much time with him as it takes to help him buy, just like the three solid days at the Coca-Cola offices. Meanwhile, pretend we are driving toward that big Coca-Cola office on North Avenue, and all these nice tire kickers are just smaller places on the route. We'll be polite and smile if they wave at us and we'll wave back, but we have a destination in mind. Or, if we wanted to just test human reactions to help us learn about the reception our product would get at Coca-Cola, we would stop at a small place and road test our product.

Also, selling is always a give and take thing. We have one of the finest displays in the whole show. The buyers are going to be attracted to it. We have a big walkway through the center display and a few tables with colorful umbrellas on them. The products we sell are top quality. So we don't actually have to go anywhere, but simply can be selective about which new people arriving should get our attention.

What's that? You ask how we are going to sell those motor homes? I don't know. That's the truth. You just got here twenty minutes ago, and maybe you think I'm the "expert." Sorry. I just started yesterday myself. I've never sold motor homes before. Yesterday? Yes, yesterday. Well, how are you going to teach me if you just got here yourself? Good question. Glad you asked. I'm not going to teach you. The buyers are going to teach both of us.

Here? In this show? While we are selling to them? That's right. And because this is true, we had better watch them very, very closely. They are our teachers.

Here comes a pair now. Wow! How about those hot pants and that bandana top? Neither item has got enough cloth in it, has it? Plenty of woman in there though, everything where it belongs and just the right size. What would you say she is, maybe twenty-five or so? He must be at least forty. They look happy, don't they? No glazed-eyed shuffling through the display with this pair. They are moving right along, and as she jiggles, a spectator bumps into a literature rack. Maybe they are buyers, if we can slow them down enough to find out.

Tell you what. Smile at them right now, even though they are forty feet away, walk toward them, and never take your eye from them. O.K.? Now catch his eye and let your bearing show you are approaching them, but not like a steamroller. Whatever else you do, don't look at this woman's body. Why? Well, you see he is holding her arm in a protective, possessive way, and look at the smile he is giving her. No, she is territory, and don't trespass, even with your glance. He sees you coming and returns your smile. Now he says, "Hi."

What? "Hi" doesn't teach us much? You don't know what to say next? Say "Hi." Then ask a question. Any question, as long as it stops them. What question? Well, how about being real polite and letting these folks know right up front that they are our teachers. People like that. How do you do that? Easy. Just like in school with a school teacher. Go ahead. You know how to do that.

"Hi! May I ask you a question?"

"What is it?"

Terrific! They stopped. They also know they are in control here. Now you want to know what the question is to ask them? Well, what are you curious about? Like, here they come, looking like buyers, in one way, but not shopping our display, just walking through it. Want to ask them about that in a nice way? Try it.

"Well, you folks look like buyers, but you haven't even glanced at our display. How come?"

Absolutely perfect! They were about to get out of sight. Questions usually get people to stop and think for a second. Also, it gives them control. They are telling you. This last point is debatable, for they are also telling themselves. Maybe the question is the controlling thing. But it needs to be an interesting or thought-provoking question.

"Oh, we've already picked out a motor home."

Now, wait. Maybe we're not lost yet. They have just proven they are buyers. And maybe they haven't totally completed the deal. Even if they have, we can learn something about preferences if we ask a few more questions.

"What kind did you pick?"

"A Golly Whiz Bang." (Sorry, 1973 was a long time ago. I can't remember the actual brand name.)

So, O.K., a Golly Whiz Bang. So what? Now what do I say? Congratulations? Or, "It's a rotten choice?" Well, maybe. But first, are you sure it's a rotten choice? If you are, how can you be? Maybe it's perfect for them. Right now, if you say something negative you might insult them. Why not let them tell us and also repeat it to and for themselves why they like that one. When they sell us on it they have to sell themselves too, and we can see how much they like it. So how about, nice and easy with a smile, ask them to sell you their Golly Whiz Bang. Let's see if they are good salespersons. That will also take some of the pressure off us for a minute. Ready? Ask them for a sales pitch.

"Why did you pick that one?"

"Well, we just got married. She has three kids, I have two, and we are going to take a long trip."

Now hold it right there. We do know that the Golly Whiz Bang is about twenty-one feet long because we spent a little time touring through the other displays. One big room and a bathroom and a small kitchen area. Bunks fold down from everywhere. So you ask, so what? Well, how about that just married bit and his protectiveness and that big smile he has for her? Looks like a pretty crowded honeymoon, doesn't it? And besides, his answer tells why he is buying a motor home, not why the Golly Whiz Bang was selected. Let's show them the real honeymoon suite. But when you speak, make them feel pleased with themselves by your words. Then the words are accepted, and since you said them, you can keep on talking some more with these people.

"Well, congratulations and best wishes! Say, I don't want to slow you down, but let me take just a second to show you something funny."

124

Why did we say funny? Well, they are already having fun, so why try to change their mood? If they had looked studious, we could have said let me show you something interesting. Whatever the mood, pick an object that fits it. Something zany. Something crazy. Something of value, something nobody in your neighborhood has got, something this, that and the other, but always something they already are.

"O.K."

Now, let's show them the thirty-footer. Take them all the way to the rear of the coach. You've got just a very short time to hold their attention so concentrate on telling it in as few words as possible. Tell them what? Tell them the honeymoon story.

"This way, miss, watch your step." Lead them in and walk quickly to the rear of the coach. See? They are following. Now how are you going to tell them the honeymoon story? Well, how about for openers, we get the five kids bedded down out of the way? O.K.? Go ahead. Have at it. After you get the kids handled, the rest of the honeymoon story will come to you, one word at a time.

"See this king size bed? It sleeps three easily. The large fold-down bunks above sleep two more. Then you come out of this room, shut the door, and here in the hallway is the bath, next to the kitchen. If the kids want a drink of water or the bathroom in the middle of the night it's right here in the hall. Then we come forward into the front compartment, shut this hall door, like this, lock it, like this, flip this sofa out into a queen size bed, like this, and sir, not one of those children have any idea of what you and mom are doing in here."

Hey, you did it perfectly! Look at his mouth drop open and his eyes dance with it! He is standing in a twenty-four thousand dollar motor home and is fascinated by a two-dollar door latch. After six more minutes, which she uses to select the cutom colors, he hands you a check. His deal on the Golly Whiz Bang "Togetherness" coach is easy for him to cancel. Congratulations! You are a salesman! Or did he just buy it? And what did he buy, the motor home or some pleasurable honeymoon nights?

You say it's fun? Sure it is! Can we do it again? Sure! Give us one more bride that sexy, one more groom with his tongue hanging out that far, a poor competitor and an ample checking account balance, and we can sell them one after the other all day long, just like cotton candy at a state fair.

But the reality is we couldn't sell just one of them in ten years. Sure, the "sales pitch" took two minutes, and the selection of options took six minutes, but he purchased in the blink of an eye. His eye.

Did we bamboozle them? Well, you gave the sales pitch. Did you make any claim that the tires would last seventeen years, or that big devil of an engine would get thirty-five miles to the gallon? Have you ever seen anybody ask fewer questions in six minutes? He had his answer, didn't he?

So slow your ego down. You are not a salesman either, any more than I am. Yet, take a second look at the examples in this book. In most cases the customer had either purchased another product already, or was mad, or had a rock solid reason in his mind not to buy, or was irritated slightly. Yet they purchased. They took a good, hard look at their own personal desires, and purchased.

You ask why we didn't look at a lot of purchase situations where it was normal? Well, we could have. I thought it would be more interesting to look at some of the fun in this selling business. And mainly it proves one thing. Even against those overwhelming odds, even with the commission in my pocket, I still never sold anything in my entire life to anybody.

Maybe it's hard for you to accept this fact. You are a grown adult and you have started selling. All that hard work talk from society and your family penetrates in deep and you feel if you are not sweating maybe you are not working. It sounds all noble to sweat, doesn't it? Almost religious. Want to hear what the Book says about it?

> "One man wins success by his words,
> another gets his due reward by the work of his hands."
> Proverbs

> "Be timid in business and come to beggary;
> be bold and make a fortune."
> Proverbs

CHAPTER 12

After "Hello", What Next?

Maybe the all time best example of what *not* to say next after "hello" happened in a small northern Florida town in the office of a farm implement manufacturer. It was one of those offices where the waiting lounge section was separated from the buyer's desk by a low railing. Sometimes cramped offices are helpful when a salesman is second in line because the buyer can be sized up as he talks with the preceding salesman. This day, in addition to the buyer and several women working at desks, the room was crowded with four salesmen waiting on our side of the railing.

The buyer had just arrived and received our names and order of arrival from one of the women. He glanced at the list, looked up, smiled and called the name of the salesman who had arrived first. The salesman stood, walked through the gate in the railing and the two short steps to the buyer's desk. The three of us waiting pretended to look at magazines and softly chatted but we were listening to see what mood we could expect in the buyer. The salesman began.

"Good morning. I'm Joe Smith with . . . uh, with uh . . . I'm Joe Smith, with, uh . . ."

"I'm with . . ."

"With . . ."

"Uh . . ."

"I'm with . . ."

As he searched his memory for the name of the company he represented, everyone stopped everything to see if he would find it. We didn't know whether to laugh or cry for him. The salesman sitting beside me began making a very faint but terrible gasping sound as he tried with every ounce of self-control to remain quiet. The typewriters stopped. Even the phone wouldn't ring. The entire world stopped momentarily. I began rooting for the man silently as though he were a horse I had bet some money on.

He backed up mentally while remaining in place physically and took another run at it, as though he had just arrived.

"Good morning. I'm Joe Smith with . . ."

Pause.

Silence.

Snicker, from one of the women.

Wheeze, from the salesman sitting next to me.

Bug-eyed paralysis in me, still undecided whether to laugh, cry or both.

The third spectator salesman had to choose between an open laugh or a cardiac arrest and settled on the former, with some restraint, risking every blood vessel in his body as he held back as much as he could.

The buyer acted like he was at the movies and intrigued by the plot.

Some more silence.

Another pause.

Silence was soundless stillness. Pause was a soundless slight shifting of weight, as though the salesman were standing on the elusive words and could thereby set them free to journey upwards to their former correct place in his memory.

"I'm with . . ."

Silence.

Pause.

"Uh . . ."

Finally the buyer put the whole room out of our misery, and his.

He said, "I have days like that sometimes. When I do, I go fishing. Why don't you go fishing and come back tomorrow?"

Smith said, without pause, "I think I will," and walked out the door.

Then we could laugh. Oh, how we could laugh. After a good long burst and a few moments trying to taper off, the buyer called me over to his desk. I straightened up my equilibrium, or so I thought, and tried to speak. I couldn't. I could laugh again but I couldn't speak. It started again and we all laughed some more. Then we found our voices and everyone commented on the incident, each person expressing both empathy for the unfortunate salesman along with amusement at his actions. The buyer asked the remaining salesmen to "please have your calling cards out and ready to read from if you get stuck." We laughed again. The phone rang. The woman who answered it reset the business mood with her efficient greeting. A fly buzzed around in circles. The water cooler gurgled. The day resumed its course as the earth began slowly revolving again.

Amusing little story, isn't it?

So what do you say after "hello"?

Ask a question. Any question as long as it gets your prospect talking. Your first task is to understand your prospect and the best way to do that is to listen to him. And since the situation has you identified as the salesman, he is sitting there waiting for you to speak. When you do, form your words into questions. Then you can relax while he sells you the exact person he is. Later you can explain your product to him with great appeal after you know what kind of person you are talking to, how this person functions emotionally, and the exact nature of his product needs.

But right now he is selling you. I know of one salesman in a jewelry store who uses an outrageous gimmick to sell watches. When he sees an honest looking man looking at the watches in the window he walks out and shakes hands with the man, and quickly slips a watch on the man's wrist, then walks back into the store. Bewildered, the window shopper follows him in. A beginning. Then this salesman lets the shopper sell him on taking the watch back. Very often the window shopper isn't a good salesman. Wild, isn't it?

If you can't figure out any other questions, just say, "How are you today?"

The big question of course, is, "If I could, would you?"

"If I could show you how to have a week in your favorite vacation spot at no cost, would you be interested?"

Try saying "no" to that one.

"Mr. Jones, if I could help you reduce your packaging costs 67 percent, would you be interested?"

"Mr. Avis, if I could show you how to become bigger than Mr. Hertz, would you be interested?

"Mr. Smith, if I could show you how to increase your production 18 percent, would you be interested?"

The answer to all these questions is usually not a plain yes. People are not so gullible as to believe in instant miracles.

The usual answer is a question.

"How can you do that?"

"Well, I don't know for sure that I can, but if I could, would you be interested?"

"I'd be a fool to say no. But I do not believe you could ever do that."

"Like I said, I'm not positive I can. But here is an example of how another company did it by using my product. Now, I'll admit your business is different than theirs, but still, the principle is still there. See, right here in this letter this man states he increased his production 18 percent. Now, I'll have to ask you some questions to see if your operation here is suitable for using this new product. For instance, how many employees do you have?"

A beginning.

When a prospect hears, instead of questions, a glib presentation of glorious claims and facts, he instinctively knows he is being sold. No one likes to be sold. Everybody likes to buy. So when a salesman asks questions the prospect feels the salesman is not just slamming away at him with a "pitch."

Salesmanship then becomes a search. And because the search is for the prospect's problems and emotions, the prospect also knows he should be doing most of the talking. People absolutely just know this by sheer instinct. The best way to get them talking is by asking questions. And when they talk they have to think.

Focus all the energy and attention toward the prospect with questions. Then word your appeal to fit his emotions.

Also, know that questions about facts always contain hidden questions about emotions. Here is an example. The following questionnaire is one used by a staff of salesmen I trained for the solar industry. As you read this questionnaire, look for four unspoken questions.

DOMESTIC HOT WATER
PRE-QUOTATION
QUESTIONNAIRE

1. How do you presently heat hot water?
   _____ natural gas   _____ propane   _____ electricity

2. What are your monthly costs to heat water?
   _____ $5-$10   _____ $15-$25   _____ $30-$50

3. How many people are presently living here?
   _____ adults   _____ teenagers   _____ pre-teens

4. Do you utilize a dishwasher? _____
   Washing machine? _____

5. Does any family member enjoy extra-long showers or baths?
   _____ No   _____ Yes
   Who? _____

6. How many bathrooms do you have? _____

7. Does everyone generally take showers/baths in the
   _____ morning   _____ afternoon   _____ evening
   _____ varied

8. How often do you presently run out of hot water?
   _____ every day   _____ very often
   _____ occasionally   _____ never

9. Why are you considering solar heat for your hot water use?

_____ friends have it and it works

_____ read newspaper or magazine articles about it

_____ PG&E recommended it

_____ want to conserve natural resources

_____ could use California Solar Tax Credit

_____ could use Federal Solar Tax Credit

_____ gas prices skyrocketing

_____ want to increase property value.

10. Have you considered any other solar companies and/or products?

_____ no _____ yes Which company? _____

11. If your house is solar-feasible and if the cost of a solar system is reasonable and cost-justified, would you consider purchasing a system today?

_____ yes _____ no

Did you spot these unspoken questions?

Do you need it? (Questions 1 through 8)

Do you want it? (Questions 9 and 10)

Will you buy it? (Question 11)

What is your emotional priority? (From inflections of voice and side comments offered as all questions are answered.)

The salesmen were trained to ask these questions in a neutral, receptive way, as though they were simply a census taker, and to avoid making any selling statements while asking the questions. Trained to listen, really listen, to the answers and moods accompanying the answer, the salesman now possessed a profile of the prospect and could add effective inflections to the sales presentation which followed.

Questions. You have no way of knowing if the prospect can use your item until he tells you. Then, and only then, you can present your ideas.

When you present your ideas, ask questions as you cover a point.

"How do you feel about that?"

"What do you think about that?"

If you notice the replies you receive to those two questions above, you will discover that the "feel" question produces an emotion and the "think" question produces logic.

If the prospect has a negative emotional answer ask a second question to receive a logical admittance and agreement. Example:

"How do you feel about that?"

"It's ugly."

"Yes, you're right. It is hard to build it pretty for the job it performs. What do you think about the durability built into the product?"

Or go on the other way when the prospect says,

"It looks too fragile."

"Yes. You are right. It is fragile, and you will need to care for it well. How do you feel about the beautiful styling?"

It is all emotional. Logic is a myth.

As you are considering what you have read, you realize that just four motives govern all purchases.

Awareness of hazard or future potential hazard.

Pride of ownership.

Desire for gain.

Imitation.

When you see a prospect, know, absolutely know, that these are the only four reasons for anybody ever purchasing anything. Word your statements to apply to these emotions. If you do not know which emotions the prospect is experiencing, ask questions until you discover what sort of person you are experiencing.

CHAPTER 13

Fabulous Pie

People invest energy in a magic illusion called "lifestyle." In-depth marketing experts make a great science of lifestyles and tailor appeals to catch the eye of every person. And because we purchase with our emotions the appeal succeeds or fails based on just one factor. We either get emotionally involved and expend some energy, or we watch in a disinterested way as others get emotionally involved. Few appeals totally miss everybody. If one person invents or designs or instigates or develops, there will be other kindred souls who will buy. The challenge in marketing is to find appeals that great masses of people will embrace. Now and then an advertiser pursues the challenge in an amusing way.

> "Once you learn to play the harmonica
> you will never be lonely again."

Can you picture this in the back of a magazine competing with eighty other small advertisements, waiting there at the bottom corner of a page to snare the eye and pierce the heart?

Alas, all products do not convey such instant magic. We must sell most of our goods in a more reasoning way. So

let's get back to our prospect who has just finished answering our questions.

Your prospect educated you about his need and desires
as your questions were answered, and also enlightened
you about the one factor in him that is the source of all
action: Energy.

He has revealed his pace—whether he likes to move
quickly or deliberately; his balance—whether he is trusting you, wary, or neutral; his style—the cheerful or quiet
way he handles himself; his direction—whether he is
positive or negative; and his self-conception—the man-
nerisms used to convey whatever he feels is relevant about
himself. You also see static information such as environ-
ment, wardrobe and other elements of personal preferences, but the key to action is the flow of energy in the
moving elements.

Trace the energy through the four natural steps of the
sale.

First, you pause to investigate.

Second, you speak to appeal.

Third, you both discuss.

Fourth, the prospect buys.

Look at that energy flow and exchange. The prospect's
energy first, your energy second, forming a common
pool of energy so the third step of easygoing conversation
can proceed, and finally, the prospect's energy buying.
Resist using your energy very much, and help the prospect invest energy, because at the end of the talk one of
you will reach for either the checkbook or the doorknob,
and the one who is up at the end will be at it.

As you begin to speak about your product you will be surprised to discover the truths about persuasiveness and so-called "powerful" speaking: that speaking is not a chore of projecting your voice and idea; that you cannot speak with conviction without first believing your listener is capable of agreement; and finally, the ultimate truth which allows and helps you to discard all nervous seeking of "power"—that inner part of your listener which you know will agree is serving as a powerful magnet to pull your idea from you. Can you feel this pull? If you can't, you didn't ask enough questions. You say you can feel it? Great! Without further ado, have at it. Nice and easy. Let that inner magnet do all the work.

Features, Advantages and Benefits: The Product

The saleswoman was tired. It was at the end of the day. She wasn't bubbling over with personality. But she did remember to ask questions before talking about an answering machine I was examining, and after she discovered I was thinking of using the machine in my home, she presented the product.

"This model has a loudspeaker, so you can hear the caller leaving the message. If you wish to speak to the caller you may pick up the phone. If you don't you can just let the message be recorded. It is your option. This means you can eat dinner when you want to instead of when the phone will let you."

Suddenly the nuts and bolts machine came alive for me! I could eat dinner uninterrupted!

Let's look at three distinct elements in her conversation and examine how these matched up perfectly with the three elements of her listener.

FEATURE:

"This model has a loudspeaker . . ."

I can see that. Now she has one part of me involved—my physical senses.

ADVANTAGE:

". . . so you can hear the caller leaving the message . . . ."

Now I understand the function of what I see. My mind is involved. But what advantage is it for me to hear the caller?

"If you wish to speak to the caller you may pick up the phone. If you don't you can just let the message be recorded. It is your option . . . ."

O.K. I understand.

BENEFIT:

"This means you can eat dinner when you want to instead of when your phone will let you."

Bingo! Now I feel it! Sold!

Notice that in any one of these three separate elements of her conversation, what she says will not stand alone. It requires all three elements to arouse desire. Also notice that she got my energy moving through all parts of myself, Physically, Intellectually and Emotionally. I became totally involved. Finally, notice how just her words alone did all the work. Her sparkle had drained away in the afternoon heat. It didn't matter. This saleswoman used the energy in the product and my energy to make the sale.

Please examine the following charts that present the dynamics of the three-step method, and see how the product is a perfect match for the prospect, element for element. And flinch if you think it is silly, but the easiest way to remember the formula is:

F.A.B. to P.I.E. = FABulous PIE

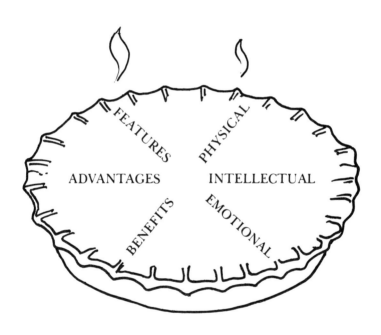

Fabulous Pie

Features		Advantages ⇨		Benefits	
Physical		**Intellectual**		**Emotional**	
What is it?		What does it do?		What's in it for me?	
How is it built?		How will it perform?		How will my life be made better?	
Is it well constructed?		Will it be durable?		Can I depend on it?	
Dry facts		Action words		Personal reactions	
"This is . . . (etc., etc.)"		"That does . . . (etc., etc.)"		"And you will enjoy . . . (etc., etc.)"	
Show it to the prospect		Discuss it		Build desire	
"This model has a loudspeaker . . .		. . . so you can hear the caller leaving the message. If you wish to speak to the caller you may pick up the phone. If you don't you can just let the message be recorded.		It is your option. This means you can eat dinner when you want to instead of when your phone will let you."	

In preparing your own worksheet, use a wide piece of paper, and:

State a fact about the product.	Tell how this feature functions, what it actually does, very specifically.	State how this performance benefits the prospect. Tell how the prospect's life is made better. Answer the question, "What's in it for me?"

The Mood of the Salesperson during the Three Steps

Calm	Active	Projecting
Factual	Descriptive	Personal
Objective	Reflective	Touching

The Mood of the Prospect during the Three Steps

Unknowing	Informed	Trusting
Undecided	Thinking	Desiring
Listening	Understanding	Deciding

This simple little chart is the key to selling when all the other principles are used. The chart pulls the truth out in a detailed way. Keep analyzing the product as you prepare the worksheet. Start in any column. If you feel good about a benefit, write that "feel good" feeling in the benefit column, and then work backwards. What advantage produced that good feeling? What feature created the advantage? List those elements.

Try using the product, and notice how little details feel good in a physical sense. Advantages will emerge, and benefits. Write it all in the worksheet.

Play the part of an intellect. Sit quietly and consider the superiority of the product in a strictly thinking way. Advantages will emerge. Write them down.

Keep it all positive. I like to keep moods positive because the prospect will let me continue in conversation with him if I "miss" on a positive statement, but if I use a negative statement and miss just ever so slightly in convincing, then the prospect has the negative he doesn't accept, and I'm the guy who said it, and I begin losing acceptance. His energy goes negative. This is important in talking about fears and hazards, and in threading through the maze of consideration about competitors. All negatives are very sensitive. If I try to use them they can easily go astray and hurt me more than help me. If I knock a competitor or hammer home a fear I am seen, very accurately, as a power stroker, and I personally become feared. A negative can turn on me in a split second like a snake at feeding time in a zoo.

I always feel that if I knock a competitor I am giving him free advertising space in my mouth right in the middle of my sales presentation. I won't do it. Instead, I present the superior features, advantages and benefits of my own product, and lift it up above my competition by saying, "This is the only product that offers these features," or words to that effect. Let the competition fall aside naturally as desire for my product is established. I'm right in the here and now and if I do my job right my competitor is wiped out automatically because the attention is all being focused on the benefits of my product.

It works the same way with fears of hazards. First present the features, advantages and benefits. Then say, " . . . and this means you will never suffer the loss of . . ." or " . . . and as you can see this eliminates the risk of . . ." and then tell about the hazard. There is a deceptively effective dynamic at work in this method. If a fear or hazard is described in advance of talking about a product, it preloads the prospect with a suppressive mood of danger. The other way, treating it like a danger "we just escaped," puts it in the past. It allows the feeling of smugness because we have this new product that eliminates the negative. So I like to point out fears after they are in the rear view mirror.

Focus on the action of the prospect using the product, and try to keep the focus moving, and not let it come to rest on the prospect. For example, I would sell a benefit of "personal growth" in an action way, trying to keep the focus on the movement of the improvement rather than the static position of where the prospect stands right now. Let's say it is a reading course. If I tell a person, "This will teach you to read," I have just embarrassed them by directly pinpointing their inability to read. But suppose I said, "This course in reading improvement works with all people, regardless of their present reading skills, and even teaches people to read for the first time, and so no matter where you are on the scale right now you become a better reader as you participate in the course." Then to convince, use a third-party reference that takes all the heat away from the prospect. "We had thirty-four people enrolled last month who could not read at all, and now they are making great strides forward and can read increasingly better." The idea in selling, to me, is to let the offering come down the street looking like a parade that people want to join.

Imitation is a powerful emotion in people, but which way are they using it? To be alike, or to be different? Watch the prospect. He'll tell you whether he feels like a sheep or an eagle. My comment is either, "This is the most popular model" or "Surely a man like yourself has urgent things to think about. This dependable and reliable model will free up your time." If I have a brand new product that has no track record, I really can't make a statement that my product is popular. But words can be used several ways, as a camera, to present the picture that exists, or as a paintbrush, to paint a picture of the future. "With so many fine benefits, we expect this to become our most popular item in the future." Same mood, two different ways to say it. Fit your words to the realities and the person you face.

Place the product in movement in the mind of the prospect. Action is the goal, not just static ownership. Even if you are selling a collectable item that sits on a shelf doing nothing, put it in motion. Instead of "You can own this," establish the mood, "This is going to give you great pleasure for a long time." One is static, the other moves. Most people already "own" an attic full of dusty junk, but the sound of pleasure is like a running brook.

Think of all these principles as you prepare a worksheet for your product listing the features, advantages and benefits. Make the product come alive for your prospect by thinking always of motion, always of pleasure or satisfaction or gratification in the continuous stream of a person's pleasure. True, you will find yourself writing static words on the worksheet because you have no prospect in front of you to supply energy to make the product come alive. Prepare the worksheet as fully as possible, and then go to meet your prospect, absorb all the prospect's energy in the third eye, and begin talking about the product with action words. "When you begin using this you will find this detail is going to produce this advantage and you are going to enjoy this benefit." Selling a man a suit? Look at the difference in these two examples. "This blend of wool and dacron keeps its press" versus "This blend of wool and dacron will not wrinkle easily as you wear it, and when you pull it out of a suitcase on a trip you can put it right on and enjoy the crisp look and feel." Put the product in action.

If I can demonstrate a product, that is the finest and easiest way to sell it, for several reasons. The prospect trusts his eyes more than my words. The demonstration lets the prospect feel it instead of "thinking" about it. But most of all a demonstration is action and action is energy and energy is the one element I must engage in the prospect.

Some salespeople say "Create desire!" as though desire is a batch of dough to mix up and roll out and cut into cookies. The truth is desire is just the forward reach of energy, and no mortal can create energy, and therefore we also cannot create desire. But we do not have to create. Selling is a simple job of utilizing energy that already exists to arouse desires that are dormant. "Once you learn to play the harmonica you will never be lonely again" does not "create". It engages the interest of someone who is already lonely. Incidentally, the ad is terrible, but it doesn't tell a lie. A harmonica is a fine companion on a rainy afternoon. Did you read that into it? Few people do because the ad is focusing on a negative.

Positive statements pick up movement as people view them from their own personal perspectives. But negative statements lock the juice down in people. I had a client who sold weatherization, and had been using a brochure showing two people wearing boxing gloves, slugging away, under the caption "Fight back on utility bills!" This was a bummer, for just one reason. It created a fight mood. Nuts! Get an antagonistic mood developed, and then sit right there in it to sell. We changed brochures, retrained the sales force, and sales zoomed. Keep it positive.

If you get around many professional salespeople, sooner or later the phrase "customer control" is going to arise. Sounds like a cattle roundup, doesn't it? Don't try it unless you are desirous of dealing with some maverick steers. You don't need to control people. Just control yourself and do exactly what you want your prospect to do. Want a prospect to read a brochure comment? Read it yourself, and hold the brochure out to your side half facing the prospect, like it is a song book two people are using, and get your own eyes in the brochure. If you look at the prospect he is going to interact with the energy of your eyes, which is a stronger energy than the energy in your pointing finger. (If this isn't true I don't want to be within a mile of your pointing finger.) The prospect always relates to the strongest source of energy. So put the energy right into that brochure with your eyes, and the prospect will be literally drawn into the brochure with you. Is this customer control? It is simply self control.

Got a loud prospect, or a customer giving you a vigorous complaint? Want to settle things down? Go perfectly still and quiet. The other person will have a very hard time dancing alone, and will take a break. Just do exactly whatever you want your prospect to do, in a courteous yet firmly inviting manner. Then wait for it. You are not a taxi driver in a hurry. You are a salesperson.

You are constantly seeking ways for the prospect to display energy. When a prospect objects to a statement, let your entire bearing show that you invite this objection. If you are writing an order and the prospect objects to a point, stop all activity to clearly show you invite all objections. Put your pen down. Turn your order upside down. Take off your glasses. Lean back. Relax. Ask, "Please tell me exactly how you feel about that aspect" or "What are you thinking?" or any completely invitational remark. To do this successfully you have to think inside the way you act outside with your movements. Don't fear interaction for a moment. There is conflict in any decision situation as the newness of ideas challenges the comfort of old perceptions. Just know that agreements forged in the heat of friendly but invigorating discussion will last until a greater truth comes along to displace them. Do not be afraid of this struggle because it is as natural as the sun coming up and going down.

Whatever you think will convey itself to your prospect in many small subliminal ways that you are powerless to stop. If you think "customer control" your prospect will feel it, one way or another. Millions of sales are lost because of this one elusive feeling in the prospect, the feeling that the salesperson is trying to "control" instead of legitimately engage in healthy confrontation of past beliefs. THINK towards the inertia of the bogged down deliberations when you get stuck, and resist the feeling that the prospect is personally being balky. If the prospect wanted to be the problem he would just dismiss you. The simple fact that you are allowed to proceed tells you that the prospect is trying to focus on the deliberations just like you are. Focus every ounce of attention on the problems, not on people. One great phrase is "How can we resolve this?" The key word is "this." Literally put the vocal emphasis on that word as you ask the question.

Prepare the worksheet well before going to sell. Use specifics. Generalities just confuse people, but specifics educate and appeal.

A newly-organized Toastmistress Club asked me to present a workshop to improve effectiveness in explaining their club to prospective members. I presented the three-step method of selling and asked the ladies to sell me using features, advantages and benefits. They quickly got the idea of "three steps" but stood, one at a time, to tell me three glowing generalities in a row. "We have an excellent program. You will enjoy participating. Your life will be enriched."

"Ladies, how many of you experienced your own personal feeling of mystery when you were first invited to a Toastmistress meeting?" Every hand shot up. It broke the ice and they began laughing. "O.K. You have been in the club for a while, and now you are relaxed and know how it feels. But your prospective new members have no idea what they will actually be doing in the club. Now, that's no problem at all if the person can be totally influenced by your own personal enthusiasm. But many people want to know up front what's in it for them besides the smiles, and just what it is that produces the smiles. Let's try it again, and this time, sell me by using some very specific details of that 'excellent program,' and then tell me the advantages and benefits." After a thinking pause they began again.

"We use good parliamentary procedure in our meetings, and as you participate you will run the meetings when it is your turn, and learn how to conduct meetings well, and this means that when there's a job opening in a supervisor's position you will be totally well-qualified to conduct excellent staff meetings."

"Fantastic!"

"We time our talks to be brief. This teaches you to organize your thoughts, and you will become a more articulate communicator."

"Fantastic!"

"We also have an impromptu topic at each meeting. Each member comments on this topic briefly. This teaches you to think fast on your feet. You will become more spontaneous and poised, and that flustered feeling will slowly disappear."

"Fantastic!"

"Fantastic!" is the prospect's line. The salesperson's lines are features, advantages and benefits. The reason the prospect's line gets crossed and into the wrong mouth is that the salesperson already knows all the benefits and already knows it is "fantastic!" But the prospect hasn't seen the show yet and isn't ready to applaud while waiting in line to get ushered into the theater. The salesperson must be willing to be locked into "the first encounter" with each and every new prospect, and let it all unfold slowly, one step at a time—one, two, three; features, advantages and benefits.

Be sure to keep including the benefit statements. If a salesperson ever feeds just facts to a prospect's mind, and those facts do not reach the prospect's heart, no decision will be made, and the net effect is identically the same as dropping coins into a drink machine and getting nothing.

You will know if you miss connecting when you face a

very vocal prospect. You tell a feature, and he says, "So what?" Next you tell the advantage, and again he says, "So what?" Finally you tell the personal emotional benefit, and that's "what" and he says, "Hmmm! Interesting!"

But few prospects give you clear feedback, so the usual rule "When in doubt, leave it out" is reversed in the three-step sales method. If in doubt, put it in, in a low key way that feels like a casual comment, with a tone of voice that gently says, "You already know this and this is just a reminder." Then ask for feedback. "How do you feel about this?"

The "winner" phrases in selling are the personal emotional benefit statements, tailored in whatever way your third eye suggests to the exact energy being displayed by your prospect. Just begin in advance of your sales contact by preparing a thorough worksheet, and then memorize every single feature, advantage and benefit. Then meet your prospect and draw out the "hot button" in his desires with questions. Your prospect's answers will be the guide for presenting your product.

Take a second to go back to page 125 where you sold the motor home and re-examine your words, reading just that one single paragraph where you began describing the king size bed in the rear bedroom. That paragraph looks odd after reading this somber chapter, doesn't it? This is because the energy of that previous chapter is different than the energy of this chapter. There we were in full swing in the energy of the show and the prospect. Here we are examining products in the abstract. Please notice this in your reading experience and in your own response with your energy. Now, that is exactly what happens with each prospect you face. Each person displays and uses energy differently. So the F.A.B. to P.I.E. presentation must vary from person to person in the variety of situations you face.

Follow that energy as it unfolds in your prospect. And when the energy curves out in an odd way, hang in there and snare it.

Sometimes the energy is buried or blocked in the prospect and you must help set it free. A woman walked into a furniture store and said, "I'm here to buy a sofa . . . [Fantastic! A guaranteed sale!] . . . and this time it can be any color except blue." Ooops! It just got complicated. Her face was contorted with determination.

"Why is blue not acceptable?"

"Well, you'll laugh, but my last four sofas have been blue, and my family has kidded me about it pretty hard."

"Yes, Ma'am." It was all I could do to choke back a laugh.

I began showing her sofas. Gold, brown, green. Plaid, tweed, brocade. But each time we passed a blue sofa, I commented.

"Pity blue won't do. That one is on special sale today."

"Shame you can't use blue. This is one of the most comfortable sofas in the store."

"I know you will not buy blue, but feel this fabric! Luxurious, isn't it?"

Thirty minutes later, sitting on a gold sofa, the determination and gritted teeth suddenly relaxed, and she smiled brightly. "Let's look at the blue sofas! I don't care what anybody says, blue is my favorite color, and if they don't like it they can move out!"

She paid for a blue sofa, then tried to thank me "for my patience."

"Forget it, and thanks for the business. Blue is my favorite color too, and I have the same difficulty at shirt racks. If they don't like it, phone me, and I'll come help them pack."

I'll bet a dollar she went home and said, "The devil made me do it!"

Pogo, the swamp possum cartoon character created by Walt Kelly, said it best. "We have met the enemy, and he is us."

Energy. Where is it? In what direction is it focused? What will it do? How can it be used to proceed? Are the product details of greater relevance to the decision than the energy dynamics? Is it of greater value to present the product than to capture the energy? It is said "It is better to give than to receive." If that means giving attention first and material goods second, is that correct? Where is the energy?

Focus on the natural energy in your prospect. A man and a woman came to a jewelry counter where I was just "watching the store" for a friend. I didn't know anything about the jewelry, but the woman did, and pointed to selections, trying them on one at a time, until finally she stood admiring herself and the latest selection of jewelry in the mirror. Before, with each selection she tried, she had asked the man if he thought it would look good with this or that dress. The man had been hesitant, unable to visualize with her, and it seemed to perplex him. But he looked well-heeled, and seemed willing to buy the jewelry, and his confusion was simply not being able to help select. I wondered if the woman would turn to the man again to ask his opinion. Time to capture the energy.

I looked at the woman. "Do you like it?"

"Oh, yes!'

I looked at the man. "Do you like her?"

Laughter.

"Will this be cash or charge?"

158

The product itself almost completely disappears in some transactions. It all takes place in the emotions of the prospect, and all concepts float from reality into imagination.

That's fabulous pie, à la mode.

These are the Rules of Energy

Don't wear yourself out. Use the other person's energy all the way.

If the energy is blocked or buried when you meet someone, help them set it free.

If a person has a weak energy signal, help them increase its strength until it can make a decision.

When two people have mixed energy that blocks each other, help it find a harmony and a straight path to a decision.

When someone has strong energy, ride it like a wave and don't mess it up.

You can present the same product to many varieties of energy you encounter.

If you personally get someone's energy confused, you owe it to them to help set it free again.

Let the most miscellaneous portion of energy make the decision if it is strong enough.

Energy that has been used once can often be recycled and used again.

Always route the appeal to energy through the emotions.

Let energy travel the path of least resistance. Make the broadest highway you can for the energy to travel.

When energy shifts, follow it.

If you wish to more fully experience the dynamics of energy, and to more thoroughly see the dynamics of "FABulous PIE," may I suggest re-reading this book? Do it this way: Print the word "Energy" on a book marker, and print below it "F.A.B. to P.I.E." Place the book marker so that those words stick up in full view above the pages, always in sight as you read. Pause as you read to ask questions about energy and F.A.B. to P.I.E.

Re-read the "sales pitch" to the hotel executive on page 101 and see that all the F.A.B. to P.I.E. involved me selling just my service. Read the words used to sell the motor home on page 125 and see that we were selling the actual physical product as we used F.A.B. to P.I.E. Read the story of the Cline Company progress, beginning on page 70 and see that we were selling neither product nor service, but instead, simple harmony, and yet see the implication of F.A.B. to P.I.E. along with the greater emphasis on the energy of the situation. Analyze all elements in this manner. Ask yourself which buying motives were being touched with the appeals in each instance.

CHAPTER 14

Getting the "Yes"

Please try to think of it in this form. The other way, calling it the "close" of the sale, begins at once to load a lot of negatives into the situation.

All of the statements, questions, answers, problems and solutions, from the first "hello" on through to this moment, when you feel your prospect is ready to buy, have been your "yes." Now it is time to write the order. In the old vocabulary of selling, this time is called the closing. Sounds like a door, doesn't it? And if it is a door, as it closes, am I inside with my prospect, or have I found myself out in the cold? Or in the old "knock 'em dead" philosophy of selling, maybe "close" means dropping the lid on the coffin to secure the fresh corpse.

It is sometimes said of a "power" salesman, "He is a strong closer." Maybe. But also, maybe this strong closer is a desperate door slammer on a very windy day or a coffin lid banger on a corpse that still has some life in it. Most of the people I've seen who were said to be "strong closers" were also weak presenters, in some way. I've talked with salesmen and retraced the path of their sales conversations with their prospects. My favorite question when a "yes" was not received is, "What did the customer say was his reason for not buying?" Now here is the funny thing. When a salesman replies two times in a row, "The customer didn't believe in the quality," I go immediately into asking the salesman to play-act his presentation with me, pretending I'm the prospect. Sure enough, right there in the early part of the sales conversation, when features, advantages and benefits are being discussed, the salesman is either not explaining well or is not pausing to get agreement on the quality features. Now, at this point when the prospect should be ready to say "yes," those old doubts still reside in his mind and cause him to say "no." If the prospect's reason for saying "no" was, "I want to check out some of the other companies before I buy," this indicates that no agreement was reached on the high standards of our company. The salesman didn't tell the company story well.

This is so predictable that the phenomenon can be stated as a solid principle backed up by an accurate mathematical formula:

Whatever important point is left out of the presentation will resurface later to block the "yes" decision.

Close minus Agreement equals No Transaction

$$C - A = NT$$

CAN'T GET THE ORDER

I know this is true after countless re-examinations of salesmen's presentations in "no" situations. So the best way to help salesmen is to re-examine the customer's no and the customer's answer to the question, "Why do you feel you wish to wait on this decision?" The help lies not in assisting the salesman in finding a better way to ask for the order, but in helping him see the weakness in his earlier statements.

Here is the difficulty in strong "closing" and weak presenting. First, the strong closer often learns to rely on his power at the end of the sales situation, and gets a little sloppy in his beginning. This works out like a dog chasing its tail because it is a progressive disease. Becoming weaker in his beginnings, the salesman now must become even "stronger" in his closing efforts.

Back in the early part of the sale, everyone was relaxed after the interest-gaining third-party reference was used and accepted. But here at the end, the prospect is facing a yes-or-no decision time. There is some natural tension as he poises on the point of decision. If he says "yes" it will change his life as it was before the sales presentation. This change is a small trauma. It's like asking Linus, the Peanuts comic strip little boy, to let go of his blanket.

Now, when is the easiest time to gain agreement on all the points about the product? Is it early, when everyone is relaxed? Or is it now, at the end, when the prospect is in the traumatic mood? The answer, of course, is in the early part of the conversation. Small ideas presented early can be accepted without threat, but here in the end it becomes clear that agreement leads to "yes" in short order. The trauma of change causes resistance. In this way, the facts which would swing the prospect to "yes" must now be presented in a clouded emotional atmosphere. The salesman ends up on his knees begging in the effort to get a point acknowledged. Earlier, the prospect would have agreed on the point cheerfully.

Also, if the prospect readily agrees on a point early in the talk, then later gives that same point as his reason for not wanting to purchase, you can gently remind him of his previous acceptance. "Mr. Prospect, you say you wish to check other available suppliers. Earlier, you carefully examined my company's qualifications to serve you well and fairly, and you agreed that this is exactly the kind of company you wish to do business with. Isn't that desire still valid?"

So the reality of the so-called "close" situation is that it is not a single asking for a "yes," but is merely the reaffirming of the "yes" that has been built into the sales presentation and previously affirmed in all the smaller "yes" responses to the smaller points of the selling conversation.

Once, when I simply asked for "yes" by taking out my pen and beginning to write the order, the prospect stated, in a jovial but firm voice, "Hey, wait! I didn't say I'd order it yet!"

I laughed and said, "True, but you didn't say you wouldn't, either. You've agreed with everything we have discussed, and I've left nothing out, so what else is there to consider?"

He laughed and said, "I guess you're right. I'll buy it."

This response indicates the satisfaction of the prospect in everything that is important to him. It is possible to ying-yang back and forth forever on a decision, and a three-day discussion could conceivably arise about a yo-yo string. What color, how thick, of what material, how braided, what length, which schoolyard yo-yo champ uses what, and why, and how much lunch money he won as a result, and where he was born and does he eat Wheaties? Then we could go into the origin of the yo-yo, its inventor, how he got the inspiration, how much money he made on it, etc., etc., etc. But if you stand in front of me with a stringless yo-yo and I show you a string that fits, is of the right length, and you accept the color of it and like the feel of the loop around your finger, my next comment is going to be, "Five cents, please." What else is important?

The asking for "yes" occurs in one of two places. First,

in some of the unusual sales incidents in this book there often was no real detailed presentation of the entire product. Yet in these instances it is clear that the prospect had his major concern satisfied and desired to say "yes." At that exact time the correct action is to write the order. This can happen in the blink of an eye. At a resort where I was a working (selling) sales manager, a woman drove up, sprang from her car enthusiastically, looked at the lake with a big appreciative smile and said, "I've got just one question." I asked, "What is it?" She asked, "Can my daughter come use the resort alone when I can't come?" I said, "Yes. Let's go over to that picnic table and fill in your membership application." A few smiles later she signed a check and walked over to the lake's edge to enjoy the day. One salesman asked, "Why did you write her application so fast?" I stated, "Because she said she had just one question, and I answered it. Why wait for twenty more questions? She was ready to join."

The other place where the "yes" is asked for is after all the customer's priorities have been satisfied and he agrees that it makes sense to him. In fact, then one of the best ways to ask for "yes" is, "Mr. Prospect, there you have it, the complete picture. Does it make sense to you?" When he says "yes," reach, without one single, additional word, for your pen, and without looking up from your order form, say, "This address is 1247 Elm," as you write it down. Then ask, "What's the zip code?" When he gives you the digits you know he is ready to accept delivery.

I dislike the word "close" because it implants the idea that the sales conversation is ending soon. This thought makes me feel like I'm running for a bus and have to get there fast before it leaves. A sales conversation has no end, no scheduled time of departure. If I see I can get a "yes" answer and the profit to me is worth the time I will spend, then there is absolutely no rationing of time.

This philosophy allows me to function in my true perspective. There is no such person as a salesman. People buy. My job is to hold up, in plain view, exactly what the prospect wants, in order that it can be purchased. So after I've held this commodity up I ask if that is the item he wanted by asking for an order.

Go back and look again at some of the sales incidents in this book. Do you get any feeling of the final question I used just before the "yes" being a question that contained no hope for additional discussion if it produced a "no" instead of a "yes"? In every instance, I still had the freedom to continue the sales discussion. As it happened, the prospect readily agreed that his concern had been satisfied.

But suppose he had just blinked and made an additional comment? If my job as salesman is merely to hold up what the prospect desires in order that it can be purchased, then all I have to do when he says "no" is to reach back into Santa Claus' toy bag for a different item. The next question is something like, "Why do you feel this is not a good purchase for you?" When he answers, his words will help me fish out a different item for him to consider. The product itself never changes, just the emotional appeal. I can reach in that bag fifty times, pull out a different emotional appeal and hold it up, and if it is rejected, I can cheerfully throw it aside and reach again. When you are dealing with people sometimes it is so confusing that it becomes like a rummage sale, and you have to sort through all of it to find the item of value. The idea is to go empty, let the third eye compute all the knowns, let yourself be influenced by your inner voice, then use the best words your inner voice gives you. But if they fail, guess what? Your gut is empty again and your third eye begins all over again.

There is a point at which it may appear "yes" is getting to be more faint as a possibility rather than an upcoming event. When this happens the action required is to get the prospect more involved. One jobber prospect, after my calling on him three times without getting his "yes," was well into our fourth consecutive conversation with the same complacency. He didn't speak much, mostly grunted at my questions, and in general appeared to be fast asleep. My questions were not drawing him out of his trance. Finally, in absolute fatigue, I said, "I'm going to leave now. But I will return next week and the next and the next, and I will keep on coming back until you tell me exactly what is so great about the line of shock absorbers you are selling. Now, you bought them and you stock them and I refuse to believe an intelligent man like you does not know why you sell them." Before he could blink, I turned and walked out the door. The next week when I returned he began on me in earnest, wide awake, ready to discuss, well, actually, more like tell me a thing or two. In the process, his personal preferences and his desires were exposed. When we discovered that my product would fill those desires better, he purchased. How else can it work?

There is no close to a sale, merely a point in the discussion when the prospect says "yes" or gives a reason for saying "no." The sale continues. In my territory when I worked for Aeroquip Corporation, the Seaboard Air Line Railroad and the Atlantic Coast Line Railroad merged to form the Seaboard Coastline Railroad. Each company had used a different refueling system, one of which was manufactured by Aeroquip. I called on them to convert the entire system over to Aeroquip's system as a standard. Buckeye, the manufacturer of the other system, also sent their salesman. For two years the Buckeye rep and I battled heads. I rode that rail system from one end to the other, talking to every man I could find who ever touched a refueling nozzle, either in service or in the shops as repairs were made. My district manager cautioned me that I might not get the order. Well, they never said "no," and I knew railroads were not impulsive businesses, but preferred to consider changes slowly, so as far as I was concerned the sale was still proceeding. Finally, we got the "yes." Two years. Hundreds of small decisions as each man in the railroad considered and cast his vote with his superior. Now someone tell me, when was that sale supposed to end?

I recently heard a dramatic story from a salesman who sold furnaces years ago in Michigan. One salesman wasn't bringing in any orders from home owners. Finally the sales manager had a little talk with him. "You are getting embarrassed about your idea of imposing on your prospects. Now, I want you to change one thing about the way you work. Tonight, I want you to give your entire presentation, get as much agreement all along the way as you can, and then, at what you feel is the end of the conversation, do not get up and leave the home. Sit there. Talk about anything you feel comfortable talking about. I don't care if it is baseball. Just sit there until the prospect tells you it is time for him to go to bed and asks you to leave. But don't you volunteer to get up and leave. You are there to spend the evening with your prospect. If they invite you to spend the night, do it."

Late that night the salesman phoned the sales manager and reported an order for a furnace. From that point on he regularly brought in orders.

The actual dynamics of the "I want to go think about it" frame of mind is that the prospect is avoiding personal confrontation with himself. The decision point in the time frame of the sales conversation is the place where he has to wrestle with himself, and he is avoiding it. He has enjoyed the salesman's visit and the interaction but now he wants to avoid the ultimate reality. There is no free lunch. Talk to a salesman and you are going to be asked to make a decision. "I want to think about it" is not a decision. Only "yes" or "no" is a decision.

I've had people tell me, "Phone me later." If it is a small deal, there really isn't much point in cluttering my future with a big list of people who all want me to phone them later. So one way to handle it is with a reply somewhat on this order: "Mr. Prospect, you have your feeling of whether you really want it or not, so let me help you do both of us a favor. Right now you are stuck on this decision. If I go away and leave you in this indecision we will have it on our minds. You will have to keep on and on wrestling with it and I will have to keep on and on checking back. Take the easy way out and tell me 'no.' Or go for what you want by saying 'yes.' Which one will it be?"

Usually, only three things can happen when a salesman asks for an order. The prospect says "yes," "no," or "I want to think about it." It really doesn't matter which one of the three the prospect says, the sale continues. The only time it fails to continue is when the salesman decides the sale is over, that there is no hope, that the door has closed. With "yes," the salesman becomes an order writer. With "no," the salesman becomes ignorant all over again, and asks a question.

"Mr. Prospect, we've talked at length about this proposal and you have been agreeing all along that this is a fine idea and that your own needs and desires are fully satisfied and enhanced by this new idea. Now you wish to hesitate in agreeing to go ahead. Would you tell me how you are feeling about it?" Note the question is not

"What do you think about it?" Thinking often produces a three-day discussion about a yo-yo string, while feeling produces an emotion. All the merchandise is purchased emotionally.

Or,

"Mr. Prospect, you've been very cordial and this whole conversation has consisted of our thinking about it, and you have generously shared your thoughts with me. Will you share your feelings again and tell me which particular aspect of our agreement needs more thought?"

Either question produces a response, and in that response, there are the exact words or implied phrases which tell the salesman exactly where the lack of the "yes" response has originated.

Sometimes a prospect is indecisive because he wants some additional logic to add to his desire. People do this in an attempt to live wisely without being governed by emotions alone. The attempt never fully succeeds, for after seventeen sound, logical reasons are found for purchasing it still will not happen until the prospect adds in an emotion. For totally wise persons, the emotion may be a combination of pride of ownership of this superior new product, desire for gain in the benefits of the product which the prospect, after endless computation, now believes will be his. This wise new prospect may also see, very intelligently, the hazard of his continued existence without the product and his awareness and commitment to excellence may tell him to purchase. Finally, he may purchase to imitate other wise pioneers from the past who are his heroes, all of whom had a keen eye for an astute and courageous new step into the unknown. Those are all emotions. Logic, all by itself, never purchased anything.

But logic is a tool we all use to allow us to trust our

emotions. It all seems to work out at decision time as, "I like it. Now is there anything in this deal that would make me dislike it later?" Sometimes people hang on the edge of a decision trying to superimpose logic upon emotions and line them both up so well that the final picture will not look like a double exposure negative. That is very hard to do. So when you are asking for a "yes" and the prospect is hesitant, you have a ping-pong game on your hands between logic and emotion. The salesman's job is to help one factor fit well with the other. If the prospect fears his money may run out if he buys the product it is the task of the salesman to present enough logic and fact to dispel this fear.

Example: "I like it, but I cannot afford this new car."

"Mr. Prospect, you said you spend an average of sixty dollars a month on repairs, and a hundred and forty dollars on gas. This new car will be repaired under warranty if it breaks down, and this efficient, smaller engine will save eighty dollars a month on your gas bill. You come out a total of one hundred and forty dollars ahead by driving this new car. Isn't that enough to let you drive the car you really want to drive?"

Or,

"Yes, I see your need to get the most you can for your money. This is the finest component you can use on the product you manufacture. This product is so well-known and respected by your customers, that adding it to your finished product gives you a very saleable advantage over your competitors, at a relatively small cost. Your image and reliability improve. Isn't this slight extra cost justified to give the image you desire for your product?"

Please note these ending sentences begin with logic and end in emotion.

Here is one of my favorite ways to ask for "yes," and the incident where I first learned it.

"First one to talk loses."

A salesman told me about this principle and I decided to try it. It made sense.

A few days later I was up in North Carolina selling shock absorber merchandisers to service stations in a major oil company franchise chain.

The company representative who was taking me around to his station operators warned me in advance. "The next dealer we are calling on is so quiet that he may never say a word to you the entire time you are there."

"You're kidding, I hope."

"No. Believe it or not, I've taken salesmen in there and he has never said one word the entire time we were there. Some days he never says more than three or four words to me when I come here alone."

"Is he mad?"

"No, just quiet. About the quietest person I've ever seen."

"O.K. Look, will you help me try an experiment with the man?"

"Sure. What is it?"

"Well, how about me giving him a real smooth presentation, whether he talks much or not. At the end, I will ask him this quesion, verbatim: 'Mr. Jones, in view of the fact that so many cars need the shock absorbers replaced, and considering the way our products fit so well into your normal way of operating, and because you stand to gain so much on our special offer today, is there any reason why we cannot deliver your merchandiser package to you today?'

"Now, when you hear that question, be totally silent. Do

not speak. Let the question hang in the air until he speaks to answer it. If the silence is awkward let it be awkward for him, not for us. O.K.?"

"All right. I'll try it with you."

We pulled into the station, got out of the car and went in to meet the prospect. When he was told my name he put his hand out. I told him I was pleased to meet him. He silently moved my hand, up once, down once, and dropped it.

I began telling him about the product right after I asked some complimentary questions about his station which he didn't answer. During my presentation I made some attempts to secure agreement on small points. He didn't answer any of the small questions so I helped him by answering them for him. Finally I got to the end of my presentation and asked him the agreed upon question, verbatim.

"Mr. Jones, in view of (etc., etc., etc.), is there any reason why we cannot deliver your merchandiser package to you today?"

The man was standing with his back to the wall where the clock hung. I glanced at it and noticed the time. Seventeen seconds later the guy I was selling with got nervous.

"It's a real good deal, Sam!"

Luck. Plain dumb luck. A car pulled in for gas and our prospect went out to service it.

I turned to my buddy for the day and said, "Look. You promised to help me with this experiment. You flinched. Now when he comes back I am going to back up into my presentation again, warm him up again, and pop the exact same question to him again, word for word. When you hear it coming bite your tongue and let's let him answer. O.K.?"

"O.K."

The prospect came back in and I replayed some of the presentation for him again.

"Now, Mr. Jones, in view of (etc., etc., etc.), is there any reason why we cannot deliver your merchandiser package to you today?"

I flicked my eyes to the clock and glanced at it again twenty-eight seconds later when my buddy killed it again with,

"All the other guys are putting it in, Sam."

Damn!

And then more dumb luck. Another car pulled in and Sam went out to service it.

I turned to my selling partner. "Here is some change. Go. Buy yourself a Coke. Carry it to the car. Sit down. Shut the door. Put the Coke in your mouth and suck on it until I am through. I am going to pull a 'yes' or a 'no' from Sam or bust my gut with the effort."

"You're kidding."

"No. I'm as serious as a heart attack. Go."

He left and Sam came back in after a few more minutes.

Back into the presentation again for a brief refresher course and a reheat of the same hash, then, "Mr. Jones, in view of (etc., etc., etc.), is there any reason why we cannot deliver your merchandiser package to you today?"

I glanced at the clock, then fixed my attention on Sam's mouth. As I stood there gazing at Sam, waiting for his first sound, somewhere, people made love. In other places, kids raised their hands and teachers let them go to bathrooms. A few hundred miles to the east the Atlantic Ocean rolled in, crashing on the shore. Cars rolled off assembly lines in Detroit, to replace others which were at that very moment gasping to a stop with ruptured engines, or wrapping around trees, to the chagrin of drivers, who were at that instant beginning the journey across the mystic river into eternity, making space for the babies who were at that precise moment filling their lungs with oxygen, to cry out in protest against their rude removal from the comfort of the womb. A mockingbird perched in a tree at the edge of the station destroyed my wandering thoughts and prompted Jones into speech.

"No, there's no reason."

I tore my eyes from Sam's mouth, looked at Sam, then glanced at the clock.

Eleven and one-half minutes had passed.

"Thanks, Sam. We'll deliver this afternoon."

Silent again, he offered his hand, then took mine, moved it up once, down once, and dropped it.

"Goodbye, Sam."

No answer as I left.

Three points:

One, I could let my mind wander. I gave the question to Sam, it belonged to him. Let him mess with it.

Two, as long as I stood there quietly Sam had only one way to deal with me, and that way was the question I had given him.

Three, people love to say "no" to salesmen. Look at the wording of my question and at Sam's response. Let them say "no." Help them say "no." Then ship them what their "no" purchased.

Now here is the single principle of fairness in asking for "yes," or if you prefer, "no." Just answer this question, reflect on it as you work, and it will give you an inner "permission" to keep on asking for the "yes." The question is this: "Am I continuing to focus upon the good points of my product and present its benefits in a helpful way with my persistence?" If the answer is "yes," keep right on asking for a "yes."

There is another way to be persistent, and when it is used it converts positive persistence into negative aggravation. A book salesman tried to use it on me once, when I was hesitant about saying "yes." He said, "Mr. Lewis, do you want to purchase these books or do you want your children to grow up ignorant? Do you care about them at all?" Bingo! Exit one book salesman. If he had said, "Chuck, think about this, these books are valuable learning tools for your growing family. You want to have these tools, don't you?" it would have been a positive. Maybe his third eye helped him change his attitude and words on the next call.

In other words, any aggravation that makes a jerk out of the prospect is a negative. Any pleasant persistence that creates a continued picture of benefits is positive. And that is the sole test of whether your effort to secure agreement and "yes" is harmful or helpful. If you are committed to helping the prospect and know your product will benefit him, hang in there and alternate your words. Ask for "yes." Get it, or if "no" is the answer you receive, ask, "Why?" then answer the objection and ask for "yes" again.

Multiple calls

When a prospect cannot say "yes" and purchase on the first call, and often this is the case for larger decisions, state positives in a way that keep on selling him while you are gone and have him ready for your return.

Some suggestions.

"Talk to your salesmen (or your file clerks, or accountants, or whoever). Our product looks good to you and me, but verify this with your people. They will have to use it. In particular, ask about this feature and get their reaction."

Make it specific.

"Compare this feature with the feature of your present product (or method of performing if no product is used). Next week, as you consider, look specifically at this area of concern. I'd like to hear your reactions when we get back together."

Or,

"Can you take an actual inventory appraisal before our next appointment so we can compare it to the proposed new inventory? I think when you do this you will see the value of this proposal."

In whatever you leave behind you, in the prospect's mind, let it be a specific, preferably the one with the most impact on the decision. Gain his agreement to perform the task of this one specific consideration. When you return, one of two things will have occurred. Either he will have done as agreed and he will have established in his own mind the value of your proposal, or he will have neglected to do as agreed.

But even if he has neglected his task, there is still a positive convincing element present in the emotions. Anything that is solid enough for you to have trusted him alone with its appraisal must surely have merit. This is an inherent fact implied upon the surface of your confident proposal of time to consider, and although the prospect's consideration was not in fact actually given as agreed, still, the positive upbeat openness of your offer has created a plus about the detail emotionally. In other words, the prospect now feels you are probably right without actually knowing it positively by having checked it.

Project ᵗhis into your conversation when you return

and let the overall climate of the talk be upgraded by absorbing this positive.

"Well, Mr. Jones, you've checked the inventory question (or with your salesmen, or whatever) and now you can see the value of our proposal. Is there any other problem we should iron out before we proceed, or are you prepared to order now?"

As the prospect reflects upon your opening statement and request for the order, if he accepts all other aspects and details of you and your offering in a positive way, he just may make a decision to accept the validity of the unchecked, unverified point also. Who checks every single detail of every single thing? No one. People usually use judgement of impression as fully as evaluation of fact. This prospect may now lean toward all the other positive impressions about you and simply trust your appraisal of the undecided facts. He is now ready to purchase.

If he hesitates, ask quietly, "How important is it to you to verify this question that you already feel is answered?"

If he says, "very important" and puts off the order, he is at least admonishing himself to get with it and get busy checking it out. If he smiles and shrugs, ask for the order. Either way, there is forward movement toward a decision.

The final factor in giving yourself "permission" to continue to ask for "yes" is simply the dynamics of human interaction. Your prospect agreed to discuss the proposal with you. For some reason, he was interested enough to engage in the conversation. He has allowed you to spend your time and energy discussing benefits to him. Now he is hesitant.

The dynamics of the search for agreement are the dynamics of the system for figuring things out. The prospect has doubts mixed with trust and wishes to observe, before deciding on his own personal truth. As a salesman, respect this process, and do one additional act. Remain in the prospect's presence as he figures it out. Memory is often inaccurate. Your prospect may, if left alone, forget the benefits of your product, or forget some specific point you made in your presentation. So you simply remain with him to assist him in reaching his truth. When it arrives in his mind, he may say "no" with finality.

If the prospect is totally uninterested he can say "no" firmly, give no reason for his response, and end the discussion. But when the prospect says "no" and you can surely sense his regret or his indecision, you can safely ask a few more questions to see if the reason for his reluctance is a problem you can solve. You are simply extending his period of observation.

When a prospect gives you a reason for declining the purchase, look at it. Place yourself in his position. Ask yourself if you would purchase if you were him. If the answer is "yes," continue to discuss the solution to his concern. If the answer is "no," you yourself would not purchase in those same exact circumstances, then simply say, "Thanks for your interest," and leave.

All rules of all games are equal and fair to all players. The prospect's final truth may be the exact opposite of your truth. If this is so, there are no losers. He has achieved his truth and you have done your best. Forget it. Walk away from it. Ask the learning questions. Learn from the experience, then forget it and move on to the next prospect. But just before you leave, ask one more question.

"Mr. Prospect, I can appreciate your reasons for not purchasing at this time. But maybe you can take just a moment and possibly give me the name of someone you know who would be interested in hearing about this product. Can you think of someone?"

"How did I do?"

Did I prejudge my prospect or myself, or did I enter with neutrality and ignorance?

Did I utilize the four points of loving people—Knowledge, Acceptance, Concern, Commitment?

Did I begin by arousing interest, activating energy through curiosity?

A good "If I could, would you?" question?
A motivating Third Party Reference?

Did I help the energy flow by asking questions?

Did I discover the "Hot Button" emotions as I listened?

Did my presentation connect directly with the "Hot Button"?

Did I get the features explained all the way through the mind to the emotions, with understood advantages and desired benefits?

Did I get small agreements all along the way?

Did I carefully absorb the energy thrust of the prospect's additional questions?

Did I answer them satisfactorily? With emotional desire building?

Did I keep all the focus in the ending discussion totally on the prospect's energy, and the reassurances of the performance and benefit of my product?

Did I honor the prospect's system for figuring things out—Doubt, Trust, Observation, Truth?

Did I help the system work for his betterment?

Slip a small tape recorder in your pocket, and record yourself on a few sales calls, for review later. Better yet, when you call on a good experienced salesman, when you finish, laugh a little, ask for a helping hand, then hand him this list and ask him to comment. Any conscientious salesman will be glad to help.

CHAPTER 15

Changing and Being Changed

A paradox within our society is focused directly upon the buying and selling of goods. As a salesman I feel the implications of this paradox in a direct personal confrontation of my habits. My life up to this point has been financed by the sale of goods. Now, suddenly, the awareness is upon me that the fouled air I breathe is a product of my productivity. The ever-growing threat of war to secure fuel "rights" (in reality merely consumption of the plunder of war by the strongest participant) is a present potential merely because I desire to ride instead of walk, to be heated rather than more fully clothed, to consume rather than conserve.

The partial solution lies in a personal realistic appraisal of individual desires compared to the overall price society must pay for my greed. When I ride you also must breathe the air I foul with my engine. If war erupts to secure fuel you must share the horror of the conflict.

In a conscientious effort, I can choose to refrain from consuming more than I must as I live my life. In this way I can express my love for myself as well as a greater collective love for all of us.

But if part of the solution is personal wisdom in individual consumption, surely the other part must be my contribution to some sanity in the collective marketplace. And here lies the problem.

As a salesman I have an effect upon the overall progress of civilization and the personal habits of my fellow man. But as a salesman, I am also lazy. I would always rather convince the prospect in front of me than invest the effort required to go find a fresh prospect.

In the quest for customers, I am lazy in another way. There is nothing so all-encompassing as the laziness of a salesman. I choose items to sell which will be readily received. Sometimes the products are new and untried, but featured in the product is a benefit with a value substantial enough to induce the prospect to become a customer. My job is simply to explain newness in such a way that it appeals directly to some age old emotions. And there is the rub, the potential failure, the danger in salesmanship, for what the public will buy most readily is not always what it needs in terms of our dwindling supply of natural resources.

The American culture has adorned itself with much whimsy and grandiose trappings of luxury beyond any reasonable, practical use. The primary function of a tremendous portion of our goods is merely to confer status upon the owners of the goods. Those with status pay a high price while those in lesser positions dream and struggle toward parity, longing for the day when the elusive product of manufacture will be achieved to elevate self positionally and emotionally on the comparative scale. To state this bluntly, we have become a nation of pretenders. Our clothes are simply costumes designed for whichever of life's parties we believe we are attending. Our cars have become either the gladiator's chariot or the elegant riding chair of a prince. Getting from point A to point B safely, economically, and quickly has taken second place in consideration as automobiles are selected as clothing, merely costumes donned to complete our fantasies. Even with smaller cars and better gas mileage we still indulge the fantasy, looking around carefully to note all our neighbors in the smaller cars before we feel the courage or the pressure to buy one ourselves.

Today the real estate market is in absolute peril, the chief danger being that castles are unaffordable, unsaleable, and the yearning masses in lesser structures are perplexed. Yet few grasp the simple fact that residents of the average apartment live a more luxurious life than the rulers of many peoples scattered throughout the world.

In the intense effort of settling this continental wilderness and forming it into a nation, we have adopted an ethic that now threatens our survival. Big is great. Bigger is stupendous, and to acquire more than a fair share is the mark of genius. And standing at the forefront of this feeling is the enormous contribution of the American salesman. And yet, he isn't all bad.

The Ivan Allen Company is the South's largest office supply firm. Ivan Allen, Jr. became mayor of Atlanta and performed with great civic spirit. His father, Ivan Allen, Sr., sold the first typewriters in the state of Georgia. He was a marvelous old man with a great love of people and a twinkle in his eye. A pioneer. Now his son, also a fine man, sells probably twenty kinds of typewriters and his salesmen number over a hundred. Down the street from Ivan Allen's store is the Hyatt Regency Hotel, designed by another great Atlantan, John Portman. Three great salesmen and renowned citizens.

But does the American public need twenty kinds of typewriters and a building whose main virtue seems to be the repeal of all previously known engineering logic? This question is too big for me, for I need neither of those items as an individual. To the consternation of the typesetter, I write with a pen. But does society at large need this excess? I can defend Portman's structure from an artistic viewpoint for it is a marvel to walk into the lobby and look to the top of the building from the atrium floor. But it is no more impressive than the average canyon, or as beautiful as a run-of-the-mill spring day in a wooded glen.

But because the wooded glen has always been there, while Portman's building is a Johnny-come-lately, we cluster in the building, praising the inventiveness of man in its conception and construction. The glen remains empty. Or so it used to be. One block of buildings was razed in downtown Atlanta and grass planted. Now more people can be found out on that patch of grass than rubbernecking in Portman's lobby.

Somewhere within, the American spirit is slowly re-examining the first pilgrims to arrive and the early emigrants toward California. We are becoming tuned in to their simpler emotions in some ways, and searching for simple, outdoor pleasures in record numbers.

The Atlanta Symphony Orchestra now finds its greatest expression in Piedmont Park. In contrast to the former starchy mood of a symphony audience in formal dress, the music is enjoyed by families in jeans picnicking on the gentle slope of a natural hillside amphitheater. Blankets on the grass and picnic baskets have replaced box seats and wine sellers. The whimsy of this marriage of serious music and festive spirit is symbolized by a few elegant candlesticks glowing and an occasional bottle of champagne chilling in a silverplate ice bucket. Atlanta has class, even in Piedmont Park.

Whereas a few years ago power boating at nearby Lake Lanier became a favorite pastime of Atlantans, now rafting down the Chatahoochee River directly into Atlanta has become the rage. On an average summer Sunday two to five thousand rafters can be counted participating. Suddenly, everyone who can walk seems to know about backpacking. Canoes have been rediscovered. Tennis has become a passion for many. America has rediscovered itself and is busy visiting lakes, rivers, parks, and mountain trails.

In cultural counterpoint, big is still great, stupendous is magnificent, the lion's share still coveted, and we are still pretending. Joggers compete for shoe ownership as well as distance. Debutantes shop in sweat pants and gold jewelry. We are still locked into our costume syndrome. Me too. I like cowboy shirts this year. Meanwhile, Portman possibly plans new architectural extravagances and Ivan Allen's store is visited regularly by even more typewriter salesmen, each with a new gimmick.

Typewriters and buildings may not be hazards to our depletion of natural resources. These examples are cited to defend our salesmanship as we relate and grow together. It is not for any one person to proclaim, but rather it is for each individual to decide what faction of our growth produces the hazard. Meanwhile, good luck and a long life to Mr. Portman and Mr. Allen.

What all this has to do with selling is very simple. We, as sellers, must evaluate the social impact upon the earth and its inhabitants when we select our goods to sell and our methods to merchandise them. We are proficient at our game and our game is to change the habits of our prospects. We do make a difference. We do change our world, one of us and all of us, changing and being changed. Because we are masters at selling each other we owe it to ourselves to be concerned about what we promote. We are going to be successful in our efforts. We must choose the direction of those efforts carefully. We must cease raping the earth to adorn our egos and cease manipulating our neighbor's ego to the extent that he must toil to rape the earth to achieve peace, for peace, individually and collectively, will never be achieved by strident measures.